TEACHING THE BRAIN
The New Science of Education

TEACHING THE BRAIN
The New Science of Education

Dr Duncan Milne

Copyright © Dr Duncan Milne 2014

First published in 2014 by Junior Learning.
Junior Learning, Inc. 19744 Beach Boulevard, #389, Huntington Beach, CA 92648 (USA)
Junior Learning UK, Room 5001, 6 Slington House, Rankine Road, Basingstoke, RG24 8PH
(United Kingdom)
Junior Learning AUS, PO Box 6163, Yatala, QLD, 4027 (Australia)
Junior Learning NZ, PO Box 28-312, Remuera, Auckland (New Zealand).

ISBN 978-0-9890586-3-6

Printed in China.

Contents

Preface

The partnership of education with cognitive neuroscience provides new and exciting opportunities for both teachers and scientists. This two-way relationship gives teachers and parents a complete understanding of what is going on inside the brain as children learn. Scientists are also benefiting. As they endeavour to answer an increasing list of questions from teachers, discussions provide a wealth of topics for future research.

There are already a number of exciting brain-based findings that are useful to teachers in the classroom. For example, it is possible to consider each learning operation, such as speaking, reading, spelling, writing and mathematics, as a series of circuits and connections across processing systems in the brain. This conceptualisation empowers the teacher to look into the brain to consider how these circuits are functioning.

Brain-based knowledge helps teachers tailor curricula and lesson plans to the needs of their children. It also supports teachers with their assessments and the development of interventions. Indeed, cognitive neuroscience has much to tell us about brains that work differently. By considering the genetic, evolutionary, and biological roots to brain differences, a complete picture is gained of why and how learning problems may occur.

Teachers can also develop the most effective interventions by understanding why and how they work. A number of these techniques will involve accelerated learning approaches, such as multi-sensory learning. Despite considerable anecdotal research showing its effectiveness, brain research has only just begun to explore the benefits of multi-sensory learning and how it actually helps the brain.

How to Use *Teaching the Brain*

This book will be useful to parents, classroom teachers and homeschoolers, as well as those working with special needs students. Over the years I have received positive feedback from a number of teachers and parents who are already using this knowledge for accelerated learning.

Teachers have asked for more. This book provides an expanded view into the learning brain, tackling all the key learning processes that a child will encounter as they begin school. Brain models have been conceptualised beyond reading to include speaking, writing and mathematics. There is also a wealth of teaching material included in the book. This information is useful on its own, but can be considered alongside brain research. *Teaching the Brain* describes systematic teaching approaches compatible with how the brain is developing.

Ten Facts about Teaching the Brain

1. **The brain is plastic.** It is not a static organ and changes throughout life. Neural pathways and connections change every time a new idea or thought is formed.
2. **Every brain is wired differently.** Learning changes the formation of our brain. No two brains are identical, not even twins.
3. **The brain is an interconnected network of cells.** How the brain is connected can explain learning. When brain cells fire together, they wire together and activation spreads across the network.
4. **There are parts of the brain that are functionally specialised.** Observation of the brain shows distinct areas that are specialised for different aspects of our cognition.
5. **The brain uses parallel processing to carry out multiple operations simultaneously.** Parallel processing is fast as there are many parts of the brain at work.
6. **The brain stores information in hierarchical form**, so that neighbourhoods of ideas, language, or thoughts can be activated to support thinking and learning.
7. **The brain integrates information across the sensors.** It can move across one modality to another by transcoding (for example visual to auditory).
8. **The blue print for the development of our brains comes from our genes.** Genes predict the types of abilities we may develop and the difficulties we may face in learning.
9. **The brain has been passed down by evolution.** It has not yet evolved for classroom education and must recycle old systems for the purposes of learning.
10. **There are a number of technologies used to examine the brain.** This research is in its infancy and there is plenty more to learn about how the brain works.

Acknowledgements

My research into educational neuroscience would never have begun without the unwavering support of my PhD supervisor, Professor Mike Corballis. I have learnt so much from his fabulous brain. I would also like to thank my other PhD supervisor Professor Tom Nicholson from education.

I am grateful for the resources made available to me from the Research Centre for Cognitive Neuroscience and the Brain Research Institute, and to Professor Ian Kirk, Dr Karen Waldie and Dr Jeff Hamm for numerous informal conversations on how the brain works. At the Mediterranean Institute of Cognitive Neuroscience, I would like to thank Professor Christine Deruelle for accepting me into her research group and a special thank you to Dr Andres Santos for collaborating with me.

Others to thank in France include Dr Michel Habib, Dr Frank Ramus, and Dr Jo Zeigler. From Harvard University I would like to thank Professors John Davis and Cynthia Montgomery for bringing philosophy into education for me. Although I never studied under them, I would like to thank Professor Stanislas Dehaene at INSERM, France, for his work on the neural basis for reading and mathematics and Professor Al Galaburda at Harvard for his revolutionary neurobiological work into dyslexia. Both of these contributions have made parts of this book possible.

I have had so much support from teachers all over the world and their advice and insight has been invaluable. In particular I would like to thank Judith Sanson, Stewart Sanson and Dr Vincent Goetry from Dyslexia International, Lorraine Paterson and Beverley Walters from NASEN, Liz Waine from PATOSS, Bernadette McLean from Helen Arkell Dyslexia, Victoria Crivelli from the BDA, Bernadette Laws from Thorley Hill SpLD, and everyone at BESA.

Thanks to the team at Junior Learning for helping bring this book together. We are so lucky to have some of the world's most creative minds working in synergy from the UK, California and New Zealand. Finally, I would like to thank Anna, my wife and business partner, who constantly gives me encouragement and support. I dedicate this book to you.

About the Author

Dr Duncan Milne is a neuro-educator. He completed his PhD in Cognitive Neuroscience and Education at the University of Auckland, New Zealand. He has worked with electroencephalography (EEG) at the Research Centre for Cognitive Neuroscience, Auckland, New Zealand, and functional magnetic imaging (fMRI) at the Brain Research Institute, Melbourne, Australia. Dr Duncan has also completed post graduate studies at Harvard University, Boston, USA, and was a visiting post-doctoral student at the Mediterranean Institute of Cognitive Neuroscience, Marseille, France.

Within the field of education, Dr Duncan served on the executive council of the British Educational Supplies Association (BESA) for five years. During this time he was a founding member of the BESA Special Needs group and served as the Chairman. He was also professional speaker with the National Association of Special Needs (NASEN) and the Professional Association Teachers of Students with Specific Learning Difficulties (PATOSS). Dr Duncan has worked at the government level and has promoted best practices internationally on behalf of UK Trade and Investment in a number of developing countries. He was the keynote opening speaker for the World Dyslexia Forum in Paris at UNESCO. Currently, Dr Duncan serves as an honorary board member of Dyslexia International and is their Director of Tools for Learning.

Dr Duncan has published numerous books and scientific journal articles in education and neuroscience. His previous book 'Teaching the Brain to Read' has an international cult following with reading teachers. More recently, Dr Duncan cofounded Junior Learning, a publishing house with a mission to create educational resources that accelerate learning and make curriculum topics accessible to all children. Junior Learning has developed a number of patents on educational innovations and supplies these resources to teachers all over the world. To see Dr Duncan's various publications or to contact him, please visit www.juniorlearning.com or e-mail him at duncan@juniorlearning.com.

1

The New Science of Education

The new science of education brings together teaching and the brain. It provides a practical junction between neuroscience and education. The workings of the brain are used to guide educational theory and practice. The purpose of this book is to explore how the brain works during literacy and mathematics, and to consider brains that work differently, such as those with specific learning difficulties (e.g. dyslexia and dyscalculia) and other learning differences (e.g. ADHD, learning delay, autism).

Research into the neural mechanisms of speaking, reading, spelling, writing and mathematics can support curriculum implementation. Brain based models will help teachers and parents visualise and conceptualise all the different learning processes that must be taught. The brain model can also be used to guide intervention programmes and support personalised learning. Although the link between education and neuroscience is in its infancy, the time is right to bridge educational practice and brain research in a way that is practical to teachers and parents, and helpful to the students they teach.

The Origins of Learning

The human brain is the world's most remarkable piece of circuitry. It has evolved over millions of years to provide humans with a system that can access information, compute a calculation or remember an event. While the brain's hardware was designed to ensure our survival in the world, the brain's software has more complex functions. The amount of information available today is increasing more rapidly than the brain can evolve to absorb it. Our knowledge base is growing exponentially. To keep up, the brain must re-cycle existing systems to perform miraculous functions such as reading, spelling, writing and mathematics[1].

Scientists estimate that language is at least 2 million years old. Our early language had no spoken component, as it involved communication through gesture. Over the course of almost 2 million years, the human brain evolved to support speech. It is estimated that speech developed sometime between 150,000 and 250,000 years ago and is believed to be an innate function of the brain, like walking or breathing. The ability to speak provides humans with different survival advantages over other animals. Spoken commu-nication frees up the hands so that working and communicating can occur at the same time. Mothers can speak to their children, while at the same time have their hands free to care for them. Spoken communication allows us to communicate at night or around corners. Today, modern telecommunications allow instant contact between people al-most anywhere in the world.

Unlike speaking, the other cognitive skills we learn at school are newer in origin. Writ-ing is only 4,000 years old. Just like the television or the radio, writing was invented as an additional means of communication. Reading and writing in mainstream schools is even newer. The development of a written communication system is so recent that the brain has not yet had time to evolve and acquire these skills naturally – that is, reading, spell-ing and writing are still skills that must be taught. The invention of writing gave birth to the cognitive operations of reading and spelling. But because today's education involves newly invented operations, there is no inherited brain capability.

In mathematics, the invention of writing has enabled us to recombine structured men-tal representations of number concepts. Reading, spelling, writing and calculating must therefore be built on existing brain systems. The brain was never designed to perform these processes and thus, they take many years and some brain plasticity to acquire prop-erly. It is not surprising that so many children initially find acquiring these skills such hard work. Nevertheless, these abilities are important, as they provide extremely effec-tive ways to expand our knowledge and intelligence.[2]

The learning brain involves utilising processing systems that were not designed to do modern day classroom activities, along with some plasticity which gives the brain flexibil-ity to make these changes. Rather than the brain being a blank slate, it is a combination of evolved processing systems that we can shape into a learning machine. Education enables our brains to do things that they were never evolved to do. At the same time, writing sys-tems have been evolving to best fit the way our brains process visual information. Writing methods have moved away from pictures towards selected shapes that are more common in the environment. Shapes such as T, F, Y, I, L are hiding in natural scenes, such as the shapes of branches, trees and landscapes (see Figure 1.1).[3]

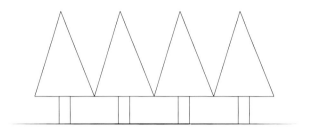

Figure 1.1 Letters are hiding in our natural environment
How many letters can you see in this visual scene? Can you see letters W, N, V, M, I, T, L, F?

Letter shapes weren't invented, but laid dormant in our brains waiting for the invention of reading and writing. By limiting the number of letters and linking them directly to sounds (or phonemes) a notation was invented that could phonologically code words. Such a change in writing was more compatible with our brain and regions where circuits could be built.

Methods of Educational Neuroscience

Our understanding of learning has increased significantly in the past twenty years. For the first time the physiological behaviour of the brain can be examined during cognitive processing. This exciting new research provides a platform for integrating findings across different disciplines such as medicine, education, neuropsychology, computer science and brain imaging. By considering learning across these different domains, a frontier emerges – the new science of education.

Behavioural Research

Cognitive research has increased exponentially in recent years. The most common method for studying learning is behavioural research. This examines the behaviour of the child while performing different tasks such as pattern recognition, single word reading, number awareness and spelling tests. Behavioural research cannot give us answers about the brain directly, as it only tests the performance output observed. However, it does allow us to answer questions about how cognition works through the observation of different tasks. Significant findings can then be repeated with functional brain imaging to examine where and when these processes are occurring.

There are numerous tests available that allow the researcher to gain an understanding of the strengths and weaknesses behind learning mechanisms. Norms from standardised tests are established across a large sample of children selected to represent the general population. Most standardised tests access competency by comparing actual skill with age-based expected skill. How is a child performing relative to others of the same age?

Other tests compare actual skill with expected skill based on a closely related skill. For example, expected reading abilities can be predicted based on spelling abilities, because reading and spelling are related. When a related skill diverges against predictions, the unusual pattern of strengths and weaknesses can be identified and the most appropriate method for teaching can be identified.

Computer Simulation

Another research technique for studying the process of learning is computer stimulation. Different theoretical models have been proposed to explain cognitive processes in the brain. Computer simulations of these theories have been created to explain how the brain works. Manipulations can also be performed using computer simulations to predict learning difficulties. For a theoretical model to be effective, it must be capable of explaining the different patterns reported behaviourally. It must be capable of explaining how the brain learns.

Neurobiology Studies

Some research can only be done by entering the brain itself. Neurobiological studies include animal studies, single-unit 'brain cell' recordings, direct brain stimulation and post-mortem studies. Animal studies on primates and other mammals have produced valuable findings on the workings of the visual system, memory, emotions and learning.

Single cell recordings are an invasive technique that records electrophysiological responses from a single nerve cell. In humans with epilepsy, electrodes are inserted into brain areas to find the location of epileptic foci. Single cell recordings have also been used in humans during mathematical processing and object recognition. Interestingly, they can now be linked to brain machine interfaces (BMIs) to control external devices such as a prosthetic limb or a computer cursor, although these are not yet available clinically as they have not been fully tested. Other animal studies map neurodevelopment of the brain in mice and rats, based on gene and environment research.

Lesion Studies

Before functional brain imaging, lesion studies were the most popular method for learning about how the brain worked. Lesions are damaged regions of the brain due to stroke or injury. By studying the behaviour of patients with lesions, their behaviour can be related to the location of damage during post autopsy investigations. This provides a unique window into the functional role of the brain area. The cognitive neuroscience of language is deeply rooted in lesion studies. They have helped scientists understand the parts of the brain involved with speech production, language comprehension, the processing of emotions and object recognition.

However, there are a number of limitations to the lesion studies method. Lesion studies assume discrete anatomical modules in the brain. In reality, the brain is more distributed and plastic. In stroke patients, other areas may take over the role of damaged areas to provide compensation, making it hard to know the exact impact of the lesion. Furthermore, healthy areas might not work properly, despite the fact that they have not been damaged, because they are no longer connected to the newly damaged area. Alternatively, more than one region may be affected, making it difficult to know exactly which part did what. Nevertheless, lesion studies still have much to offer neuroscience, especially alongside the development of new brain imaging techniques.

Functional Brain Imaging

Modern technology allows scientists to actually look inside the brain and watch it at work. Experiments can test how the brain goes about doing different things. For example, the brain's activity can be monitored as it solves a problem. By using functional imaging to look inside the brain, neuroscientists can begin to understand how the brain learns, how every brain is different and what approaches are best for learning. By separating out the components behind learning, neuropsychologists can explore the most effective ways to teach the brain in an effort to make learning faster and easier. Specialists can also develop techniques for understanding brains with learning differences, such as the dyslexic brain or the ADHD brain.[4]

More recently, functional brain imaging has become a popular technique for examining learning in the brain. Functional brain imaging can be used to test how the different sub-processes involved in cognition interact within the brain. Popular methods include electroencephalography (EEG), magnetoencephalogrpahy (MEG), positron emission topography (PET), and functional magnetic resonance imaging (fMRI). Each of these techniques has its own advantages and disadvantages based on image quality and cost.

One question which brain imaging techniques have enabled scientists to answer is: 'When do changes associated with reading a word occur in the brain?' Temporal resolution is knowing when a change is occurring in the brain. It allows the investigation of different time windows during reading. For example, EEG research shows that accessing a word from the brain's letterbox happens between 150 and 250 milliseconds after the word has been presented. Sounding out words is slower than accessing a word and occurs 300 to 500 milliseconds after a word is presented.

EEG measures brain wave patterns by placing electrodes on the scalp. Participants sit in front of a computer monitor and perform different reading experiments that have been time-locked into the EEG recording procedure. From here, brain waves can be averaged across hundreds of trials and brain responses to different types of words can be computed. By varying the types of words used in the experiment, the different sub-processes of reading can be manipulated in the brain. For example, high frequency words (such as was, that, and) can be accessed rapidly and directly, whereas nonsense words (such as minlop, trusnap, hinu) require longer processing times to decode the unknown word.

Figure 1.2 Electroencephalography
Electroencephalography or EEG involves placing electrodes on the scalp to record electrical activity from the brain. Although the electrodes are placed across the entire scalp in an effort to localise the origin of electrical activity, the best resolution from EEG is the exact timing of when changes are occurring in the brain.

The disadvantage of EEG is that it gives poor spatial resolution relative to temporal resolution. Spatial resolution allows us to know exactly where in the brain these differences are occurring. MEG works on the same principles as EEG, but is also equipped with a giant magnet to co-register where changes are occurring in the brain. Other researchers have used EEG in an fMRI scanner to collect both spatial and temporal information. An advantage of the fMRI approach is the excellent spatial information provided. Unlike,

EEG, fMRI works by calculating areas of activation based on changes in blood flow and oxygen levels. Subtractions are often used to isolate the process being studied.

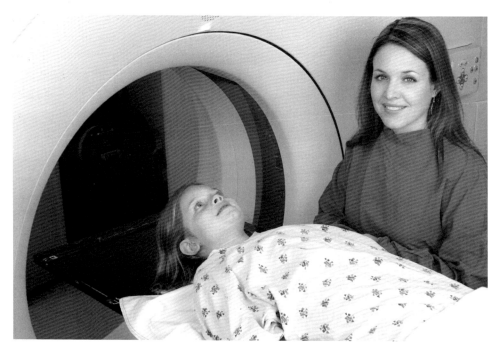

Figure 1.3 Functional Brain Imaging
Functional brain imaging such as functional magnetic resonance imaging (fMRI) is non-invasive and safe to use with children. It records the oxygen consumption in the brain and is an excellent technique for working out where a change is occuring in the brain during cognitive processing.

An interesting example of group subtractions is research into illiteracy. Adults who never went to school (illiterates) have been compared to adults who did attend school (literates) with functional brain imaging. Illiterates and literates were asked to complete a task requiring non-word repetition. Non-words are words that don't exist, such as minlop, hunnip, and reptot. Illiterates had trouble repeating these non-words, supporting the fact that going to school and learning to read increases their awareness of sounds within words. The literate brain activated more areas of the brain than the illiterate brain, especially in language regions of the left hemisphere. Even visual areas lit up, despite the fact that they were not necessarily required for listening to non-words.

Perhaps visual areas play a role in supporting the sounding out of words? At a structural level, the corpus callosum which is the nerve bundle that links the two hemispheres, had thickened in the literate subjects. Overall, this research shows us that going to school and becoming literate changes both the functional and physical properties of the brain.

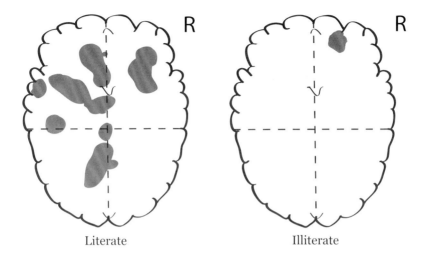

Literate   Illiterate

Figure 1.4 The Illiterate Brain
Comparison studies of illiterate (those who never went to school) and literate show differences in brain activation patterns. By going to school children develop connections across the left hemisphere to perform tasks such as phonological awareness and sounding out words (Castro-Caldas et al, 1998).

The human brain is made up of billions of interconnected brain cells. Connectionism can explain how the brain operates and learns, based on an almost infinite number of connections that can be formed between brain cells. Neurons working on their own are slow and transmit information at around ten milliseconds (about a million times slower than a computer chip). However, when millions of neurons are combined, the brain becomes very efficient, only taking one-sixth of a second to recognise a face.

Connectionism explains how specialised regions of the brain communicate with each other. Both within and between brain areas, there are connections, which create an information processing matrix. These networks of connections provide feedback loops, with ancillary support for learning.

Tractography combines brain imaging (MRI) with computer image analysis to study the patterns of water diffusion in the brain in an effort to work out how areas are connected to one another. Bundles of fibre tracks that connect regions of the brain are shown to diffuse water asymmetrically enabling their structures to be mapped. In the brain, there is a complicated network of short, long and looping bundles of fibres between regions. Although they can be studied post mortem, Diffusor Tensor Imaging (DTI) allows the study of these fibre tracks in the living brain.

About the Brain

A high level of specialist knowledge on brain anatomy is not required for understanding the practical significance of brain-based learning. Nevertheless, it is useful to familiarise with brain facts, areas and simple terminology, before explaining how it all works. Learning processes like speaking, reading, spelling, writing and mathematics involve complex neural circuitry linking specialised processing areas that reside predominately in the left hemisphere of the brain. Language itself is normally formed in the left-brain (in around 95% of us). A number of regions in the left hemisphere are 'bolted on' to the language system for tasks such as reading, spelling, writing and mathematics.

While the left hemisphere is almost always dominant in language functions, control over the right hand is typically dominant for writing. This is because the brain is cross wired, giving most of us better control of the right side of the body. But there are also same side connections, which ensure that each side of the brain is capable of sending and receiving information to both sides of the human body. Furthermore, the two hemispheres are connected together by a thick bundle of nerves called the corpus callosum.

The corpus callosum ensures that information can flow left-to-right and right-to-left. The left brain / right brain dichotomy is in many respects an oversimplification as the corpus callosum allows us to use both our hemispheres as an integrated whole. One can't simply switch a hemisphere off. When it comes to learning we spend a lot of time in our left-brain, but undoubtedly receive some support from our right-brain.

The brain consists of four lobes and a number of internal, mid and brain stem structures. Our senses feed into the brain which provides us with centralised control. The brain coordinates responses to changes to the environment. It weighs about 1.5 kgs (3 lbs) and has between 80 and 120 billion neuron cells.

The left and right cerebral hemispheres are the largest part of our brain. They are almost symmetrical and can be neatly divided into the four lobes: frontal, parietal, temporal and occipital. There is also a structure behind the brain stem and below the cortex called the cerebellum.

Frontal Lobes

As their name suggests, the frontal lobes are positioned at the front of the brain. They contain three major divisions: prefrontal, pre-motor and motor. The pre-motor and motor areas are in charge of muscle movement, including speech production and output. Demand on working memory is also demonstrated in this left frontal area. The prefrontal area is involved in higher order functions such as planning, reasoning, judgement, impulse control and memory.

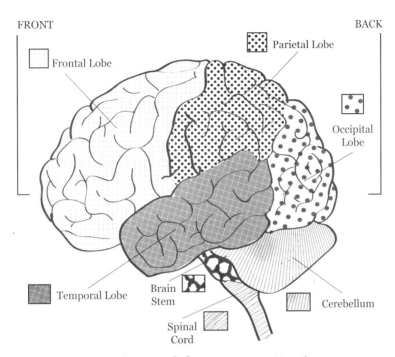

Regions of the Human Brain

Figure 1. 5   The Human Brain
The basic anatomy of the human brain has been divided into four major regions: frontal, parietal, temporal and occipital lobes.

At a higher level, it can predict the actions of our behaviour and ensure they fit to our social norms. The prefrontal areas are also believed to be involved in long term memory and linking these with emotions. The frontal lobes reach their full maturity in the 20s and slowly decline after the age of 60 at approximately 0.5% per year.

Most of the dopamine sensitive neurons are housed in the frontal lobe, making it responsible for reward, attention, planning and motivation. The prefrontal cortex is tightly connected to the limbic system (a reward system that works beneath the cortex) and this may explain why we feel rewarded after solving a problem.

Parietal Lobes

The parietal lobes, behind the frontal lobes and above the temporal lobes, are involved with integrating sensory systems, movement and space. The parietal lobe contains the somatosensory cortex which runs along the border next to the frontal lobe. This area receives touch signals from all the parts of our body.

Along the back of the parietal lobe is a dorsal stream which runs up from the occipital lobe, telling us about visual objects in space. Often referred to as the 'where' stream (where objects are placed within space) or the 'how' stream (to explain integration of motor and space, such as the grasping of an object). The parietal lobe integrates movement of the eyes, arm and hand with visual information. The parietal lobe houses the concept of numbers and this area is involved in mathematical functions.

Temporal Lobes

Below the parietal lobes and between frontal and occipital lobes are the temporal lobes. The temporal lobes are involved in hearing, both speech and auditory signals. High-level functions include comprehension and naming. The underside of the temporal lobe has specialised function for visual recognition making up part of a 'what' stream. Specialisations include face and word recognition and the processing of scenes and objects. Deep within the temporal lobes lie the hippocampi (part of the limbic system). They are crucial to memory and help convert short term memory into long term memory. Thus, the temporal lobe is important for conscious memory of facts and events.

Occipital Lobes

The occipital lobes sit at the back of the brain and are involved in visual processing. After visual information has entered the retina, it passes to the thalamus, a walnut sized structure that sits above the brain stem. The particular part of the thalamus where visual information enters is called the lateral geniculate nucleus which then connects with the help of magnocellular cells to the occipital lobe, with both forward and feedback connections. Visual information in the left field passes to the right occipital lobe and visual information in the right field passes to the left occipital lobe. After visual information has entered the occipital lobe into an area called the primary visual cortex it can begin projections.

The dorsal stream projects to the parietal lobes for information on location or motion and a ventral stream projects to the temporal lobes for information on form and object recognition.

Cerebellum

The cerebellum is a separate structure of the brain that sits behind the occipital lobe. It is involved in motor control and contributes to timing and coordination although it doesn't initiate movement. The cerebellum is connected to the sensory systems of the spinal cord as well as the brain itself. It may also be involved in cognitive processing such as language and attention.

Brain-based Models

The following chapters explore the learning brain in terms of speaking, reading, spelling, writing and mathematics. Brain-based models will be used to explain these processes at a conceptual level. A common theme across all of these operations is the existence of dorsal (upper) and ventral (lower) circuits that are utilised for different aspects of the cognitive process.

Dorsal circuits involve more of a computation, manipulation and sensory integration at the smallest unit (for example, trans-coding a letter from visual to auditory). Ventral circuits are different. They are more involved with memory, recall, and links across whole forms of pronunciations, objects and meaning. Ventral circuits are a lot faster than dorsal circuits as they access information rather than compute it.

The interplay of dorsal and ventral learning circuits across the different regions in the brain provides a powerful insight into learning. This knowledge, combined with behavioural observation in the classroom, provides a comprehensive picture of the learning process.

2

The Speaking Brain

Speaking and listening forms the foundations for communicating with other people. There is little doubt that the brain is genetically pre-programmed for language and babies are ready to communicate from the moment of birth. A few days after birth they can distinguish between 'ba' and 'ga'. They see and hear people and objects in their environment and make appropriate cries, coos and gestures. Language is developed on this early ability to communicate verbally and non-verbally. A rich environment of words, sounds, rhythm, and expressions from birth is crucial for language development.

The Development of Speaking

Infants have early skills for acquiring language. When they listen to speech in their native language they activate regions on the left side of their brains. Genetic studies have revealed a left-brain dominate gene for language which is only present in humans. A larger left-side for temporal (middle/side) regions of the brain can be observed clearly with brain imaging in the first months of life. This asymmetry is also observed in adults. As it exists in infants, this is not a result of learning and the environment, but pre-designed brain architecture for language.

When infants listen to speech they activate the left side temporal region, in comparison to music where both sides are activated. In the temporal lobe, activity is enhanced by the mother's voice.[5] This enhancement is most noticeable in areas involved in phonological processing.

Phonological processing is concerned with the sounds of the spoken language. When first exposed to language, infants have to learn to distinguish different sounds and to break them up into smaller more meaningful units. A mother's speech stream is continuous (there are not large pauses between words) and infants will need to develop a system for breaking up the speech stream into words before they assign meaning to these words.

The fact that phonological processing areas are activated by a mother's voice as early as 2 months suggests an important role of the mother's voice in the early acquisition of language. Indeed, infants are faster and better at learning words when they are spoken to by mother rather than a stranger. The clarity of a mother's speech has an impact on an infant's ability to hear sounds in words.

The language brain begins to develop when we are very young. From birth to the age of four years old there is a 'window' for developing language. In cases where children have not been exposed to language by the age of four, the ability to acquire normal fluency is lost. Bilingual children have an advantage in learning their second language when exposed before the age of four and if they do then less brain resources are required to speak the second language. It is also believed that phoneme acquisition occurs before the age of four and after this age we are limited by the number of phoneme sounds that we know. From here we have to map spoken phonemes onto our existing phoneme structure. This is why non-native Asian speakers of English can have problems with the /r/ sound.

Unfortunately, a number of children start school without extended vocabulary and communication abilities. Disadvantaged children may only have a third of the vocabulary of their peers. Language skills are important for learning and making friends and become pre-requisites for reading, writing and learning mathematics.

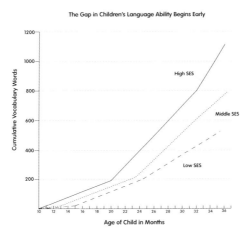

Figure 2.1 The Language Gap Begins Early

The socio-economic status of a child's family has a great effect on their vocabularly development. By the age of 3, children from high socio-economic families have almost twice the number of words available to them than their low socio-economic peers (Hart and Risley, 2005).

How the Brain Speaks

Three processes are presented in the study of psycholinguistics as part of a tripartite architecture of language. These are phonology, meaning, and syntax. There is good reason to believe that phonological (sound), semantic (meaning), and syntax (structure) are all happening together and supporting one another within the front of the brain during the unification of speech. Information regarding these core components of language feed forward from the temporal lobe across two major circuits.

Dorsal Phonology Circuit

The temporal lobe connects to the front of the brain by a large dorsal fibre bundle. This fibre bundle is an important linguistic pathway for phonological processing and is considered essential for speech development and the acquisition of spoken vocabulary. It is already present in 4 month old infants.[6] Acoustic speech signals are stored in the temporal lobe which are connected across this fibre to articulatory representations in the front of the brain.

The smallest unit of sound is called a phoneme and languages have different inventories of phonemes to make up their words. During the babbling phase young infants continuously tune their production towards the phonology of their target language. Syllables are clusters of phonemes (such as 'cat') and this sound level is proposed to be an important unit for breaking up speech stream into manageable chunks for analysis.

The temporal lobe contains information of phonological neighbours (words that sound similar to the target word, such as hat and bat) both at the phoneme and the syllable level. These associations are useful and support the acquisition of new words. This dorsal phonology circuit becomes the basic neural mechanism for phonological short term memory when learning a new word or phrase.

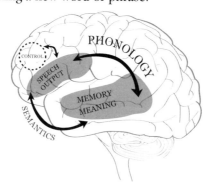

Speaking Brain

Figure 2.2 The Speaking Brain
Two major circuits are described for the Speaking Brain. A dorsal circuit involved in phonology and verbal memory for word sounds, and a ventral circuit involved in binding words and meaning.

Ventral Semantic (Meaning) Circuit

There is a second fibre bundle, a ventral circuit, which also connects the temporal lobe to the front of the brain.[7] While the dorsal circuit is strongly left brain dominant, the ventral circuit is present on both left and right sides of the brain. The ventral circuit has been shown to be involved with access to meaning.[8]

Before speaking, ideas can be formulated in the temporal lobe and transmitted to the front of the brain, where the plan of speech is carried out. This ventral circuit enables us to map meaning onto sound when speaking. Meaning is assessed sequentially, driven by the time course of the input. The comprehension process comes from the retrieval of meaning, transferred to the front of the brain via the ventral circuit to plan the speech. Here, in the front of the brain, a unification workspace is working away to piece together these components, creating the whole utterance of a phrase. It is in the front of the brain where meaningful elements are combined to form larger spoken structures such as phrases and sentences. Often, English words have more than one meaning, so the appropriate meaning will be selected based on the context of the conversation. Speech binding is also happening simultaneously across the dorsal circuit at the level of phonology. Words patterns that sound right are unified together into phrases.

Finally, syntactic structure is stored in memory in the temporal lobe. Syntax structure covers the rules and principles that govern a language. This relates to the correct order for parts of speech (such as verbs, nouns and adjectives). Chunks of syntactic structure can be retrieved and unified according to these rules. There is some debate whether syntax involves a secondary pathway of the dorsal circuit or both of these circuits working together and current research will investigate this further. The regional specialisation of the front of the brain shows speech binding of phonology at the top of the left front section, syntax in the middle, and meaning at the bottom.[9]

The biggest challenge for the front of the brain on completing this speech unification or binding process is time. Auditory processing is a lot slower than visual processing. The front of the brain must work efficiently to draw all of these factors together into a multi-word utterance. Indeed, the front of the brain has been shown as an important area for sustaining information during a transient event. It is this working memory capacity that enables the unification of pieces of information passed forward from the temporal lobe for the production of speech. The left front of the brain recruits information from the temporal lobe and unifies this into multi-word utterances with the help of its working memory.[10]

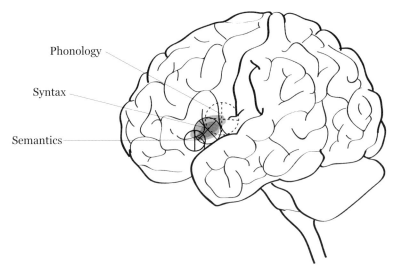

Phonology

Syntax

Semantics

Figure 2.3 Gradient of Speech Units
In the front of the brain there are different speech processing specialisations for phonology (sounds), syntax (sentence structure), and semantics (word meaning).

Attention Control Area

A further region in the front of the brain (above the speech binding area) is the attention control area. This area provides attention control during speaking and listening. The language system during conversation involves communicative intentions and actions. It enables us to speak when we observe something appropriate, or to take turns during a conversation. In the case of bilingualism, it enables the selection of the correct language for use. Compared to monolinguals, bilingual children develop greater attention focus and distraction resistance. Brain imaging data comparing bilingual and monolingual children shows increased activation in the prefrontal cortex (the attention control area). This area is connected to the speech binding area in the front and to the memory systems of the temporal lobe. It is involved in verbal action planning and attention control.

Very young children are not able to attend to what they are doing and listen to language at the same time. This is because their attention control area is underdeveloped. Around the age of four, most children will be able to attend to simple activities while listening. The attention control area will continue to develop throughout maturity (into the young twenties).[11]

Lesion Studies

A way to explore the proposed neurological model of language is to consider how damage to regions involved in this system would affect language processing. Damage to the temporal lobe has long been associated with auditory comprehension deficits. Patients with receptive aphasia cannot understand the spoken words of others. They can however speak fluently, albeit with some meaning problems such as leaving out key words, substituting words or inventing words. Although speech is correct, language content is not. These patients have damage to memory systems in the temporal lobe, but no damage to the speech binder in the front of the brain.

Patients with expressive aphasia find it difficult to initiate speech and their speaking is non-fluent and broken with little grammar or sentence construction. They do retain some comprehension, but this is at the single word level. These patients have damage to the speech binding centre in the front of the brain, but have no damage to the memory / comprehension systems in the temporal lobe.

Expressive Aphasia	Receptive Aphasia
Broca's aphasia (non-fluent aphasia): Ah... Monday... ah Dad and Paul [patient's name]... and Dad...hospital. Two... ah doctors..., and ah... thirty minutes... and yes... ah... hospital. And, er Wednesday... nine o'clock. And er Thursday, ten o'clock... doctors. Two doctors... and ah... teeth. Yeah, ..., fine. (Goodglass, 1976)	**Wernicke's aphasia (fluent aphasia):** Examiner: What kind of work did you do before you came into the hospital? Patient: Never, now mista oyge I wanna tell you this happened when happened when he rent. His - his kell come down here and is - he got ren something. It happened. In thesse ropiers were with him for hi - is friend - like was. And it just happened so I don't know, he did not bring around anything. And he did not pay it. And he roden all o these arranjen from the pedis on from iss pescid. (Kertesz, 1981).

Figure 2.4 Expressive and Receptive Aphasia
The two most common aphasia are Expressive (or Broca's) Aphasia and Receptive (or Wernicke's) Aphasia. Expressive aphasia affects the ability to speak fluently and involves damage to the front of the brain. Receptive aphasia affects the ability to speak with meaning and involves damage to the temporal lobe. There are a number of less common aphasias involving damage to these regions and/ or connections between them. They include: conduction aphasia, anomic aphasia, global aphasia and isolation aphasia. Aphasia normally develops from head injury, progressive illness, (such as dementia) or stroke.

Finally, patients with conduction aphasia have comprehension of what they hear but have serious difficulty repeating what is said. They can speak, but will frequently make phonological mistakes such as swapping phonemes around in words (velatision vs television). Although they are aware of these mistakes, they find errors difficult to fix. The reason that comprehension of speech is preserved is because the speech binder, the memory system and the ventral circuit are all intact. The lesion in these patients with conduction aphasia is to the dorsal circuit involved in encoding phonological information for speech production.[12]

Teaching the Speaking Brain

Speaking and listening begins from day one. Knowledge of the baby and sensitive observation to interpret what the baby wants, needs and feels can be reflected back in simple language. For example, 'you are feeling happy / sad / angry / tired', 'you think that's funny', 'you don't like it', 'you want the...'.

Time spent looking after the baby (such as nappy changing) is an opportunity to interact through language and form a positive relationship. Speak to babies before carrying out physical care tasks. For example, 'I'm going to help you put on some clean clothes', 'I'm going to wash your face.'

Babies must be given plenty of time to respond to interactions as it takes them time to organise the muscles in their faces to make their responses. Their responses may be coos, smiles or other facial expressions. There are a number of books available for reading to babies. Select a mixture of images including cartoons and photos. You can also make books for your baby and include familiar objects and people.

As infants develop speech, they should be encouraged to talk during play. By acknowledging all efforts at communication it shows that the child is valued. This will help build a positive relationship and support the child's independence and self-confidence. Use positive language and behaviour with, and in front of, children. Let children know of changes to the day's routine. This will help children to understand what will be happening and what the expectations of them will be (a visual timetable can be useful to support this). Support language development by ensuring the child's attention is gained before giving instructions. By using the child's name first, the child is more likely to realise that he or she is being spoken to.[13]

Teaching the Ventral Meaning Circuit

Babies are learning to comprehend language before they can speak. They will naturally learn to speak just by being surrounded in a language rich environment. Talking to babies early on is the only way they will learn language. Young toddlers like to look at images or objects that we name. Ten month-year-olds are listening into our conversations and trying to learn words. They are guided by how much they like objects and naturally assume that the word spoken by the parent goes with the object they find interesting. By the age of one they are able to recognise mispronunciation of words they know (tog for dog). At eighteen months a child's development changes and they are now capable of tapping into the parent's knowledge of words and to use their interest as a guide.

Think carefully before asking questions. Questions can be used to extend the child's thinking and learning, or simply to test. Testing young children by asking questions that you already know the answer to does not help support language development as much. Questions that are merely testing, e.g. 'What colour is it?' or that invite simple 'yes' or 'no' answers can interrupt the flow of communication and stilt natural conversation.

Children respond better to comments on their activity, e.g. 'You have made a very tall tower'. The commenting approach encourages the child to talk and keeps the child's attention on the task. Give plenty of time for children to respond. The child needs to process the adult's language, think about what they would like to say and then formulate the words. Young children who are just learning these skills need longer time. If children aren't given enough time to respond, the adult's language will dominate the conversation and will discourage the child from talking. Help children to resolve disputes and problems during play with the use of language. As children become more proficient with speaking they will be more likely to draw on their language skills to settle problems rather than use physical force. Language can help to acknowledge the problem and support the children to find a solution based on their ideas.

Children benefit hugely from exposure to books at an early age. Right from the start, lots of opportunities can be provided for children to engage with books that fire their imagination and interest. They can be encouraged to choose and peruse books freely as well as sharing them when read by an adult. Enjoying and sharing books leads to children seeing them as a source of pleasure and interest and will later motivate them to value reading.

Figure 2.5 Speaking and Listening Game
Say My Name is a "who am I" game where children take turns asking questions to work out the object on their Name Frame.

Teaching the Dorsal Phonology Circuit

Infants have a unique ability to discriminate speech-sound (phoneme) differences. Phoneme sensitivity is lost as they develop because the brain becomes specialised to process the phonemes of the native language. Eight month-year-olds start developing phonological (sound) forms of words and can recognise these without necessarily knowing their meanings. This familiarity in itself supports language development. Singing songs and rhymes are an important part of language learning. Be sure to include multi-sensory experiences such as action songs in which the children have to clap hands, pat knees and stamp feet or move in a particular way.

Rhyming books can be read with plenty of intonation and expression so that the child can tune into the rhyme of the language and the rhyming words. I spy games can be used to identify a beginning sound. For example, 'I spy someone whose name begins with sss.' Practice making various sounds with your voice. In conversation, model the correct pronunciation of the word. This means that if a child says, 'It's a dod', the adult – rather than drawing attention to the immaturity – will say, 'That's right, it's a dog'. Children can be taught oral blending (bring sounds together) and segmenting (separating components) of the sounds in words.

Children may also recognise alliterations (words that begin with the same sound). Exploring the sounds in words can occur as opportunities arise throughout the day as well as in planned parent-led sessions. Children's curiosity in letter shapes and written words can be fostered to help them make a smooth transition into reading and writing.

Figure 2.5 Rhyming Bingo Game
Rhymenoceros is a rhyming bingo game designed to support phonological assembly. Up to four children can play and support each other in finding the common rhyming sounds within words.

Teaching Syntax

At around two years of age, children may start attempting to use pronouns, adjectives, prepositions or nouns together. For example, 'Dada bye-bye' or 'me milk.' As a child's language develops, they will learn to express themselves more effectively through the use of appropriate syntax (how words form together in sentences) and grammar (classes of words, forms and functions).

Parents can model the correct use of syntax to help children. For example, it is common for four-year-olds to apply the rules of grammar across all verbs and add an –ed ending such as 'I ranned'. Here, a parent should positively model the correct way, 'that's right, you ran very fast', but they don't need to ask the child to repeat the correct sentence.Rather, the more times they hear the correct use of syntax and grammar, the more likely they are to adopt the correct structures.

Avoid responding in baby talk as this teaches the child that incorrect syntax is acceptable. Always respond as an adult. Play language games involving speaking in sentences. Use sentences to describe objects. Provide open- ended prompts 'What is the mouse doing?', 'The cheese is...', 'the mouse is...'. Scaffolding sentences gives children opportunities to use the correct syntax / grammar. Read books to children so they can hear correctly modelled sentences in terms of syntax and grammar.

Figure 2.7 Speaking and Listening Dice
Roll A Story dice let children group ideas and concepts for speaking activities as well as for written expression.

Summary

The key objectives for developing speaking and listening skills are to make sure that children have built a good stock of words, have learnt to listen attentively, and speak clearly and confidently. A good vocabulary of words builds up their ventral 'meaning' circuit. They should also have an awareness of sounds in words and be able to manipulate those sounds during games. These activities build up the dorsal 'phonological' circuit.

Finally, young children should use correct syntax structures in their sentences and pick up these structures from modelled sentences provided by teachers, carers and their parents. Children's early interest in literacy can be stimulated by exploring play, story, songs and rhymes and by providing lots of opportunities and time for talking about experiences and feelings. Sharing and enjoying a child's favourite books will also contribute massively to a child's developing literacy. Together, these skills (and underlying circuits) will provide the best foundation for developing reading, spelling, writing and mathematics when they begin school.

3

The Reading Brain

Reading is the cognitive process of converting written text into meaning. It gives us an important means of sharing information and communication. The process of reading is complex, as the brain must receive text information into the visual system and convert this information into sounds and meaning. When you read you are using your previous knowledge of written words as well as the rules of letter-sound conversion. These two distinct processes are represented by a dorsal and a ventral reading circuit in the left brain.[14]

The Process of Reading

Advances in neuroscience and modern brain imaging techniques have enabled scientists to begin unravelling the mysteries of the reading brain. Although evolution plays an important role in the development of the speaking brain, the reading brain is different. Reading has not been around long enough for the brain to evolve specialist reading circuits. By utilising speaking circuits, along with a 'bolt-on' visual identification system capable of processing words, the human brain has always had the potential for reading. Indeed, all over the world, across the various and different languages and scripts humans read, the same neural circuits are involved in processing the written word.

The Fovea in the Retina

Reading begins when words enter the retina in the eye. A central area called the fovea has high resolution cells which are perfect for processing letter and word forms. The reason we track during reading is to bring words into the fovea field. To do this we move in small steps called saccades. When you watch someone's eyes as they read text you will see the jerky movements that they make as they bring words into the fovea. At about 100 milliseconds after a word first appears on the retina, activation can be observed in the back of the brain in both the left and right hemispheres at the occipital pole. Just 50 milliseconds later, information sorting has begun where words are now activating in the left hemisphere. Interestingly, the opposite is shown for face recognition where a switch to the right hemisphere is observed. The corpus callosum is the large bundle of nerve fibres that facilitates this inter-hemispheric transfer.

The Brain's Letterbox

Visual information flows on a ventral stream from the occipital lobe to the base or underside of the temporal lobe. The ventral visual stream is divided within itself into different visual categories. Houses and landscapes are processed closest to the midline (centre of the brain), followed by faces (moving outwards). On the outer most side are objects and tools. Written words sit between face recognition and objects / tools.[15] This is where the brain's letterbox resides. It is not surprising to find faces, words and tools in the same neighbourhood as they have a bias towards the fovea (part of the eye for fine grained processing).

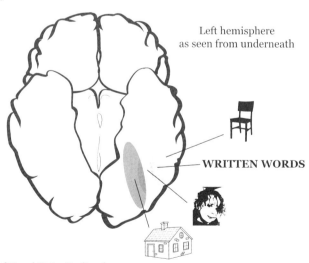

Figure 3.1 Gradient of Visual Units Outlined.
Underneath the brain in the back of the left hemisphere, visual processing regions work to recognise objects quickly. Each region is specialised for recognising certain objects. For example, houses and landscapes are recognised more towards the centre of the brain. Written words are recognised between face recognition and object recognition (such as chairs or tools) (Ishai et al., 2000).

In comparison, landscapes and houses form another neighbourhood as they prefer the periphery of the visual field. From birth, these regions are already biased towards different visual details. As letter information moves from the retina to the occipital lobe, it continues along a pathway to the letterbox area. Words can be represented in a variety of forms, from handwritten to a variety of different fonts and in lower or uppercase. The big challenge for the letterbox is to processing all these inputs of different written forms. This is called the invariance problem. The letterbox must access each letter string despite the incredible variability that letter shapes may take and it must do this incredibly fast. As visual-letter information enters the letterbox it must find a single mental address for each word despite the variability.[16]

Scientists first discovered the letterbox area when studying patients post-stroke who lost the ability to read. Damage to this occipital-temporal area of the brain results in a condition called alexia.[17] Alexia involves blindness to letters and words, without impacting on the reading of numbers, suggesting distinct processing pathways between digits and letters. Patients with alexia can continue to express themselves with rich vocabulary and can also write words, but they can't read the words they write. Here, the motor memory of the written word is saved as it is in a distinctly different location to the letterbox (where the visual memory of the written word resides).

The brain's letterbox has successive levels of letter coding. Letter coding is organized hierarchically across the occipito-temporal cortex. At the back of this region the simplest, single letter coding is engaged. Moving forward, clusters of letters, chunks, syllables and finally whole word forms are represented, all interconnected to one another according to the hierarchy. While the reading brain can process letter by letter, it can also treat groups of letters as whole units without having to pay individual attention to each letters that comprise it. Just as there are two major circuits in the speaking brain, there are also two major circuits in the reading brain. The treatment of letters as a whole word-string or individual letter-by letter-processing is the principle junction where the two reading circuits first divide.

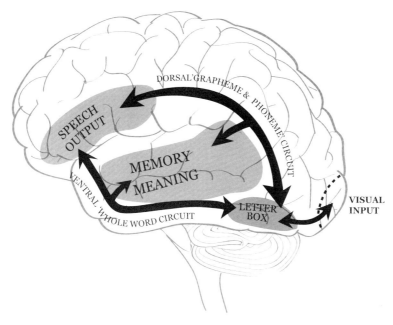

Reading Brain

Figure 3.2 The Reading Brain

The reading brain also engages two important circuits. A dorsal circuit that can convert letters to their corresponding sounds, and a ventral circuit involved with direct recall of whole word pronunciation and meaning.

Dorsal Grapheme-to-Phoneme Circuit

A dorsal circuit passes letter information forward to a 'trans-coding centre' in the mid part of the brain (super temporal gyrus) which then connects forward to the front of the brain (as described in the previous chapter). This enables letter information to be connected with the corresponding sound (or phoneme). The process, referred to as grapheme-to-phoneme conversion, starts around 225 milliseconds after a word first appears on the retina and continues until about 400 milliseconds. It involves trans-coding as 'visual' letter information from the back of the brain is mapped onto 'sound' letter information from the front of the brain. After letter-sound compatibility is reached, the forward circuit linking to the front of the brain (which belongs to an articulatory or phonological loop) provides working memory or storage space for these sounds. Blending of these sounds then occurs across this frontal circuit of the brain as sounds are merged together to create syllables and words. Once the whole word has been correctly decoded and blended, access to the pronunciation and subsequent meaning can be achieved.

Ventral 'Whole Word' Circuit

In contrast to the dorsal circuit which works from letters to sound, the forward most part of the letterbox area can respond to the entire word. Each word has a different threshold for firing based on its frequency. The length of the word doesn't seem to make much difference in terms of processing time when processed by the ventral circuit. As long as the word has less than seven letters then the processing time remains constant. This is because parallel processes in the letterbox enable component letters to be recognised at the same time. Once the visual word form is recognised, a projection is made forward to frontal regions charged with pronunciation and temporal regions involved with access to meaning. These activations occur between 250 and 300 milliseconds.

Regions at the front of the temporal lobe are believed to be in charge of combining words into sentences based on meaning. When reading a sentence that doesn't make sense, the brain will respond to the word that doesn't belong. These are known as semantically incongruent words. For example, when reading the sentence 'She drank a cold glass of nails,' it is the word 'nails' that produces the inconsistency. 400 milliseconds after the word 'nails' is presented, the temporal cortex responds: 'wait a minute, something's not quite right here', and a negative electrical potential is produced. Information flows forward and backward across the ventral circuit. Meaning will prime words in the brain's letterbox at the back of the brain and pronunciations in the front of the brain.

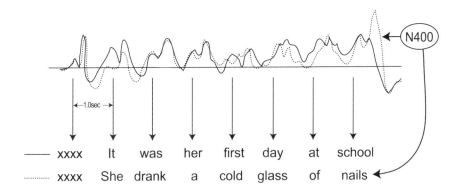

Figure 3.3 Semantically Incongruent Words.

Read the sentence: 'She drank a cold glass of nails'. Do you notice anything wrong? The word 'nails' does not fit the meaning of the sentence. EEG research shows a marked negative electrical potential at 400 milliseconds after the word 'nails' is presented, demonstrarting that the brain can use the context of a sentence to help with reading.

Access to meaning during reading comes from connections made from the letterbox to the front/side temporal lobe. The temporal lobe is not fooled by orthographically related pairs that are not semantically related (such as car/carpet). Rather, words with semantic or meaning association (such as table/desk, teach/teacher) activate the front/side of the temporal lobe. These temporal regions probably don't access meaning itself, but facilitate dispersed activation across the cortex in an effort to compose the meaning. The meaning of numbers will activate parietal parts of the brain, whereas colours will activate those visual areas involved with colour processing. Each diverse assembly of neurons that activate supplies a fragment of the meaning that is derived.

Stages of Reading Development

Three stages of reading have been used to describe the acquisition of reading. They are not discrete stages and children will move gradually between them. These stages are referred to as logographic stage, phonological stage and orthographic stage.

Logographic Stage

When children first learn to read they may begin to recognise simple words (such as stop from stop signs) by the whole word shape, before any instruction in what sounds the letters make has been given. This type of reading, referred to as the logographic stage, involves remembering words based on their visual characteristics. This pre/early reading stage involves both the left and right hemispheres, as if words are recognised as objects. For example, the word 'tall' contains letters that are tall, allowing the word shape to be recognised based on its characteristics. Children may learn the word bed as it looks like a bed with two bed heads.

Figure 3.4 Logographs

Children begin learning simple words based on shape during the logographic stage. For example, the word 'tall' can be learnt simply by remembering that the letters it contains are tall. The word 'bed' can be remembered because it looks like a bed with two bed heads. This is called direct learning and can occur before any instruction in letter/sound relationships has been provided. Instead, the brain is memorising words and accessing them directly.

Phonological Stage

Through explicit instruction in synthetic phonics, children will begin to develop the dorsal circuit for reading, linking the letterbox to the 'trans-coding centre' in the upper temporal region. As there are more phonemes than letters in the English language, a compromise is reached where letters are grouped to represent particular sounds (such as oo in food or oy in boy).

Once children have been taught systematically how the grapheme relationships of English map onto phonemes they will be able to decode transparent words (words which are phonologically accurate). As children decode words for the first time, they can access a new word's pronunciation and subsequently make a 'whole word' entry into the brain's letterbox so that the word can be accessed rapidly the next time it is seen, without the need to sound it out. After the rules of synthetic phonics have been taught, reading can use grapheme-to-phoneme conversion to sound out a new word. The dorsal circuit gives children an effective method for reading new words.

This self-teaching philosophy enables them to become independent readers, in so much as they can decode unknown words. At this stage, reading time is related to the number of letters in a word as children must decode through the word to read. This word length effect is observed in young readers and takes years before it diminishes.

Orthographic Stage

As reading matures, it typically favours the ventral circuit as this provides fast and direct access to word meaning. This happens around the start of adolescence as a vast lexicon (or visual word store) has been established for known words in the letterbox. As a word is read, its lexicon is activated, along with visually-similar word neighbours based on their frequency. Here, letters are assessed in parallel, accounting for an increase in speed and a reduction in the word length effect. Activation in the letterbox area increases as reading improves and shows a stronger left brain lateralisation. Letterbox activations even correlate more closely to reading performance than chronological age. However, it must be emphasised that both dorsal and ventral reading circuits are always simultaneously activated during reading.

Phonological information based on the sounds within words is readily available. Sounding out a word is often the most effective circuit available when reading a new word and this phonological information can guide the correct pronunciation. If sounding out a word is performed within the context of reading (rather than isolated single word reading), then meaning can also help in the search for the correct pronunciation. Meaning on its own may lead to ambiguity (such as reading dinosaur for the word tyrannosaur) but with the help of phonology (/t/ /y/ /r/...) the two reading circuits can work harmoniously to access the correct pronunciation.

The ventral circuit involving direct access to meaning also has advantages over the dorsal circuit for certain words. For example, homophonic words (such as made and maid) do not have their meaning ambiguity resolved by their phonology. Thus, sounding out the word in isolation will not necessary provide direct access to the correct meaning, whereas placing it in context will.

Finally, there is another group of words called irregular words that do not have direct letter-to-sound relationships. The rules of grapheme-to-phoneme conversion do not always apply in a number of English words. Words such as colonel or yacht cannot be read accurately without prior knowledge of the pronunciation. Although these words do contain some phonological regularities, they need to be learnt directly (or memorized) as the rules of letter-to-sound in the dorsal circuit do not apply to the irregular component of the word.

Adult Reading

Adult readers have an extensive knowledge of words, so the ventral circuit can directly access meaning for most of the words read. This becomes the most effective way to read, as it is fast and accurate. The brain doesn't want to decode every word as this would take too long. Besides, it doesn't need to as these words are already sitting in the letterbox. It is only when coming across an unknown new word when the dorsal circuit is used for decoding, by mapping graphemes onto their related phonemes.

Scientific experiments have established that the ventral circuit is significantly faster than the dorsal circuit and that the letterbox grows stronger as reading matures. In a research setting, the dorsal circuit is required for reading nonsense words (such as groob), as these words are not stored in the letterbox. Interestingly though, there is still activation in the letterbox, even for nonsense words. This is because the letterbox accesses visually similar words which helps the brain know firstly that the nonsense word follows the orthographic patterns of English (in comparison to random letter strings sdfgfx which don't activate the letterbox) and secondly, are there any neighbourhood words with similar patterns which can be broken up to help read the unknown nonsense word. Often a mixture of nonsense words, high frequency words and irregular words are used in brain imaging experiments to test the function of dorsal and ventral reading circuits.

Teaching the Reading Brain

Teaching the reading brain involves mass functional changes. Despite every brain being different, all have the same architecture for where the reading circuits are to be established. Through reading instruction a neural hierarchy is established to order letter patterns and their related speech sounds. Unlike speaking and listening skills which develop spontaneously by being surrounded by language, reading instruction requires more explicit instruction.

Teaching the 'Ventral' Meaning Circuit for Language

The 'ventral' meaning circuit for language connects a word's meaning in the temporal lobe to its articulatory output in the frontal lobe. Infants are acquiring ten to twenty new words a day by their second year. They begin school with several thousand words. Verbal fluency is a measure of the number of spoken words a child knows, recognises, and uses. Having good verbal fluency is an important building block for learning to read, as speech is the output that it produces during oral reading. Parents and teachers have a responsibility to explain the meanings of words children don't know and should encourage the use of new words. All communication, including reading to children, helps to develop verbal fluency (ventral circuit) and the basic grammatical rules of speaking in the English language (syntax).

Figure 3. 5 Sequencing Cards
Sequencing Snakes are a set of sequencing cards that have a sequence pattern on one side, and the body of a snake on the otherside. By turning the cards over the child can see if it is correct as the parts of the snake will match up. Sequencing activities provide good opportunities for speaking and thinking.

Teaching the 'Dorsal' Phonological Circuit for Language

A major predictor of future reading achievement is phonemic awareness. When children gain phonemic awareness they are capable of breaking up pronunciations into phonemic units of sound (dorsal 'phonology' circuit). Behaviourally, they now have an understanding that spoken words are made up of smaller units of sound that can in turn be manipulated. They also become aware of different units of sound. The largest unit of sound within a word is the syllable (e.g. caterpillar: cat/er/pil/lar), followed by the sub-syllabic level of onset/rime (e.g. /c/ - /at/). The smallest unit is the phoneme (e.g. /c/ /a/ /t/).

Phonemic awareness is specific to individual phoneme units of sound (/c/ /a/ /t/), while phonological awareness also includes larger units of sound within words (/c/ /at/ or /cat/ /er/ /pil/ /lar/). Developing an awareness of sounds within words is useful when learning to read as it prepares us for breaking up and sounding out words (decoding).

Phonemic awareness can be taught with fun games and activities. Picture or object groups can be used for the 'I spy' game. Children can identify a picture that they know the initial sound of, for example, ball, and say: 'I spy with my little eye something beginning with the /b/ sound.' The 'I spy' game teaches children that words are made up of different units of sound and how to isolate these sound units within words. Nursery rhymes are an excellent way to begin developing phonological awareness as they provide repetition, rhythm, and rhyme. Children can hear similar sounds embedded over and over in the words of nursery rhymes.

Rhyming bingo games let children compare the sounds behind pictures to see which pictures share the same sounds. Children do not need to 'pass' one unit of sound before gaining experience with another. Larger units of sound may be easier for some children to initially acquire, since the smaller phonic units can be harder to isolate. Children can develop syllabic awareness by clapping out the syllables of a word, for example, by clapping out the syllables in butterfly – but/ter/fly.

Phonemic awareness will continue to develop as children learn to read. The introduction of letters gives children a visual code to understand how sounds are represented in words and the effects of manipulating sounds in a multi-sensory way. As children gain a greater understanding of letters, they will gain a great appreciation of speech sounds and vice versa. Thus, there is a reciprocal interaction between understanding speech sounds and their corresponding letters. The more knowledge, skill and awareness we acquire of one, the better our understanding is of the other.

Figure 3.6 Letter Sound Bingo Game
Silly Soup is a letter sound bingo game that encourages children to listen to the initial sounds of words and match them to objects that share the same sound. The game is self-correcting as each puzzle piece has a unique shape that will only fit onto the correct soup bowl.

Teaching Dorsal 'Grapheme-to-Phoneme' Reading Circuit

The dorsal 'grapheme-to-phoneme' circuit runs from the letter-recognition units of the letterbox in the back of the temporal lobe, to the trans-coding junction at the top of the temporal lobe where it meets with the 'phonology' dorsal circuit. Teaching the dorsal circuit requires phonics instruction in the letter-sound correspondences of the English language.

The key to effectively teaching phonics is to systematically follow a progression from simple elements to the more complex aspects of phonics knowledge. Best practice is fast paced, interesting, and multi-sensory, drawing on a range of stimulating resources. It should be delivered in relatively short, discrete daily sessions.

As our writing system is alphabetic, beginning readers must be taught how the letters of the alphabet represent the sounds of spoken language. The letters may represent sounds individually or in combination and can be blended (synthesised) to read words or broken up (segmented) to spell words. Blending and segmenting are taught as reversible processes. Children must learn to process all the letters of a word both within text and in isolation. These skills can be introduced in a well defined, systematic sequence that builds on knowledge of letter sound relationships.

The teaching of letter names is sometimes left until after the sound of letters has been learned to avoid confusing children. However, research indicates that children often learn letter names earlier than they learn letter sounds and that five-year-olds who know more letter names are likely to know more letter sounds. Letter names may be easier to learn than letter sounds because they are syllables rather than phonemes. Given that children will meet many instances outside as well as within their school where letter names are used, it makes sense to teach letter names early. It appears the distinction between letter names and sounds is easily understood by the majority of children.[18]

Words that have already been learnt can be broken up into chunks to help learn new words. Research shows that children develop this skill very early in reading acquisition. An analytic phonics approach enables the brain to draw on common letter/sound relationships embedded in word families.

The reading brain can analyse new words using common letter groups and their phonological relationships obtained from previously learnt words. Analytic phonics places fewer demands on working memory as the co-articulation (the joining together of sounds) has already been made, providing further scaffolding during synthetic phonics instruction. For example, it is easy to decode 'crash' as /cr/ /ash/ from other words (such as crab, crane and cash, ash) are easy to recognise, whereas synthetic phonics takes more processing to decode /c/ /r/ /a/ /sh/. Analytic phonics should not replace synthetic phonics, but support it.

As children are introduced to new letter sounds (synthetic phonics) they can consider families of words that contain those letters (analytic phonics). Some words with ambiguous vowel sounds are initially predicted from known visually similar words. For example, the word 'flow' is pronounced /flow/ like the words tow and grow, and unlike the words cow, now, and down.

The use of visually similar words and words patterns within those words helps us work out at a sub-conscious level the most likely pronunciation based on the relationships of neighbouring letters to the ambiguous vowel sound. Put simply, it helps organise the hierarchical structure of the letterbox. Neighbourhood words with similar letter or sound patterns are activated to support the reading process. These activations feed in to support the dorsal 'grapheme-to-phoneme' circuit. This occurs at the levels of visual analogy, rhyme and meaning (morphological).

Moveable letters can be used to construct new words. CVC words (consonant-vowel-consonant) are easy to manipulate as they are closed syllables, make the short vowel sound and contain simple letter-sound rules that are easy to follow (for example pig, dog, cat). The –VC component at the end of CVC words in the rime stem. Children can see that words ending in the same stem share the same sound pattern. The initial sound can then be manipulated to make new words. For example, change the /m/ sound in mat, to a /b/ sound to make bat.

Children can also perform other operations on CVC words with moveable letters. Letters can be brought together to blend sounds, know as co-articulating, and separated to explain segmenting, deleting or isolating. Children can also substitute letters (with other letters) to make new words. For example, swap the /e/ sound in net with the /u/ sound to make nut. Once children have mastered these operations, they become aware that words are made up of different units of sound that correspond to different letters and can in turn be manipulated. Word-level work using moveable letters can combine synthetic phonics, analytic phonics and phonemic awareness into one lesson.

Figure 3.7 Learning Landscapes
Learning landscapes are a teaching resource from the Rainbow Phonics programme that encourages children to build words based on a systematic synthetic phonics progression. Each learning landscape is numbered and follows a particular order as letters are introduced week by week. The progression only presents words with letters that children have already learnt, meaning that all words are decodeable.

Teaching the Ventral 'Whole Word' Circuit

The staged model of reading acquisition shows that as children acquire the dorsal reading circuit (grapheme-to-phoneme conversion), they will have the skills required to build their ventral circuits. By successfully decoding an unknown word they can make a direct entry into their letterbox so that it is available for instant access next time it is read. However, there are some cases when the ventral reading circuit is required to directly learn words.

It is generally accepted that reading and writing is difficult to learn in English because the relationship between sounds and letters is more complex that other alphabetic languages. There are a number of irregular spellings and words containing these patterns that are required to be learnt by rote. Such words are referred to as exception, irregular or tricky words. These words can be taught directly as they are not phonically regular, such as 'the' and 'was', but occur frequently in children's reading. They can be learnt individually as well as in the context of real text.

Phonics Progression

Letter sound instruction should follow a progressive order that reflects the complexities of the English spelling system and builds upon the relationships that children already know. The simplest and most frequent letter-sound correspondences can be introduced first to give the child confidence in working with a small group of letters to decode new words.

The systematic progression will work week by week, slowly bring in less frequent graphemes (such as x, y, z), complex ones (such as ch, sh, th), even more complex ones (igh, ee, oa) and ambiguous ones (ow, oo). Children can be introduced to new graphemes alongside familiar words and build these words using colour-coded moveable letters. They can be exposed to decodeable words, phrases, sentences and even texts, so long as they have fidelity to the systematic progression. Access to meaning makes the task of learning phonics relationships more practical and useful.[19]

Progression 1: Speaking and Listening

Time spent listening to children talking to each other, and listening to individuals without interruption, helps students use more and more relevant language. Waiting time is constructive as it allows children to gather their thoughts, think about what is being said, and to frame their replies.

Parents and teachers can model good listening by making eye contact with the speaker, and by asking the right questions that an attentive listener might ask. Finally, parents and teachers should provide good models of spoken English to help young children enlarge their vocabulary and learn how to structure comprehensive sentences, speak confidently and clearly, and sustain dialogue. Throughout Progression 1 they should experience a wealth of listening activities, including songs, stories and rhymes.

Children need daily speaking and listening activities matched to their developing abilities and interests. Such activities will include the discrimination and production of the sounds of speech. Oral blending and segmenting sounds in words will support the development of phonemic awareness and the later introduction of letter patterns. Whilst recognising alliteration is important as children develop their ability to tune into speech sounds, the main objective should be segmenting words into their component sounds, and especially blending their component sounds throughout a word. Exploring the sounds in words can occur as opportunities arise throughout the day. Children's curiosity in letter shapes can be fostered to support a smooth transition into Progression 2 when the first grapheme-to-phoneme conversions are introduced.

Progression 2: First 20 Letter Sounds

The purpose of Progression 2 is to introduce at least 20 letters and to move children from oral blending and segmentation to blending and segmenting with letters. Children should be introduced to CVC words for reading and spelling either using moveable letters or by writing the letters on paper or on whiteboards.

During Progression 2 they can also be introduced to high-frequency 'exception' words: the, to, go, no. Teaching materials must follow the order that letters are introduced where suitable words have been selected because they comprise of letters that have already been taught. Practice words are used for blending during reading and segmenting during spelling.

Progression 3: Next 25 Letter Sounds

Progression 3 is designed to introduce a further 25 letter sounds. The goal at the end of this progression is to have letter representations for at least 42 phoneme sounds. Children will continue to practice CVC blending and segmenting. They should know all the letter names. They will continue to learn to read and spell exception words: I, into, we, me, he, she, be, was, no, go, my, you, her, they, all, are. By the end of Progression 3 children should be able to decode 38 of the most frequent words, such as 'will, with, that, this...'.

Progression 4: Adjacent Consonants

By Progression 4 children will be ready to learn adjacent consonants (or blends) such as 'tr, dr, gr, cr, bl, sp...'. They will learn that two consonants can be blended together to produce beginning sounds for CCVC words and final sounds for CVCC words. Word lists will contain suitable words with adjacent consonants and some multi-syllable words.

High frequency words containing adjacent consonants can be introduced: just, went, help, children, from. Further tricky words can be practiced for reading and spelling.

Progression 5: Vowel Patterns

The purpose of Progression 5 is to broaden knowledge of graphemes and phonemes for use in reading and spelling. Children will learn new graphemes and alternative pronunciations for the graphemes they already know. Some alternatives may have already been encountered in the high-frequency words that have been taught.

Children will become faster at recognising graphemes of more than one letter in words (digraphs) and at blending the phonemes they represent. Suitable words and sentences are used in accordance with the final progression, so that children are familiar with the letter-patterns introduced. The remainder of high-frequency and exception words are also presented. (Refer to Appendix 1 for Phonics Progression).

Teaching Reading in Context

Children need as much exposure to text as possible when learning to read. Contextual reading also provides an exciting platform for teaching phonics skills. Children can be encouraged to use their newly taught phonics skills to decode new words with the help of the context of the story. Furthermore, high frequency words and irregular words are easier to learn in context where their meanings can be established.

Decodeable Books

Decodeable books are books written with words that have phonological transparency, so that phonics strategies will be effective when reading unknown words. The phonological structure in decodable books can also be linked according to a synthetic phonics progression, where text is compatible with the letter sounds that children know.

Each book is designed to incorporate regular text, which children can decode using the phonics skills they have secured. This enables them to benefit from quick wins in practising phonics skills and gaining confidence from reading a book. Using decodeable books as part of a phonics programme does not preclude other reading.

Indeed it can be shown that such books help children develop confidence and an appetite for reading more widely. There is no doubt that the simple text in some recognised favourite children's books can fulfil much the same function as that of decodable books. It is possible to use these texts in parallel and decodable texts should not deny children access to favourite titles, particularly at the point where they need to read avidly to hone their skills.

Figure 3.8 Decodeable Books
Word Farm and Word City are decodeable books from the Rainbow Phonics Programme (includes 12 books). Again they follow a systematic approach where each book only covers letters that children have been taught and new letters are introduced week by week throughout the progression. The use of decodeable books also provides an opportunity to introduce high frequency words (such as at, is, in, the) which are difficult to teach in isolation and favour being introduced as part of meaningful text.

Guided Reading

Guided reading is reading instruction for small groups of children who are reading at a similar level. During guided reading the other children in the class are engaged in other literacy activities or independent reading. Once children have acquired early decoding and language skills they can begin their own attempts at reading new texts. The teacher listens to the group read a story, providing support when needed.

Children can be directed to different aspects of the story to ensure they are following the meaning as they read. When a child comes across a word that cannot be read, the teacher then guides him or her to use an effective method for deciphering that word. Importantly, the first approach is to sound out the word, decoding all the sounds throughout the word and then blending these sounds together. Letter-sound prompts can be used to demonstrate the key sound. For example, when reading the unknown word sheep, ask what sound sh makes, then use the word ship as an example – ship, can you hear the /sh/ sound in the word ship. Now the ee, how do we sound ee out? And so on... If the vowel sound is ambiguous, such as oo, direct the student to a similar word that follows the sound. For example, reading the word cook, point to the sound /oo/ as in book (not /oo/ as in food). Hopefully, when they read future words (such as hook, look, or took) children will be able to use this strategy to help them decode the new word. After successfully decoding an unknown word, the entire sentence can be re-read to maintain comprehension and fluency.

Finally, if the word is an exception word, such as the word 'was', continue with the phonics first approach directing them to the first sound /w/ and the final sound /s/. These sound clues may be enough for them to be able to access the word, however if not, you can explain that the 'a' actually makes an /o/ sound because it follows the w. This may help them when decoding new words like wash and watch that also follow this rule. If children are really struggling with exception words then guide them to the regular parts of the word and then give them the entire pronunciation so they can learn the entire word for future reading. Often it is a good idea to refresh the common exception words before reading a story or to discuss more difficult words. Having difficult words fresh in working memory can support fluency during guided reading. Guided reading texts should be selected at an appropriate reading level where children can read most of the words (90-95% accuracy), otherwise they may become frustrated and meaning will be lost.

Independent Reading

Independent reading allows children to read for pleasure by themselves and should be encouraged. Reading materials available should include a range of fiction and non-fiction titles, designed to stimulate interests. The approximate reading level is above 95% accuracy.

Fostering motivation is an important part of reading instruction. A child's reading is associated with two types of motivation: intrinsic motivation and extrinsic motivation. Intrinsic motivation involves engaging in reading for personal interest, exploring the new world of reading and discovering exciting topics of interest. Intrinsically motivated children gain a sense of pleasure by being involved in reading. When faced with difficulties they are self-determined. They persist and receive great enjoyment from the conquest of a challenging task. Intrinsically motivated children invest a great amount of time in reading as they are rewarded with cognitive and emotional satisfaction. Variables such as curiosity and involvement are used to measure intrinsic motivation. When curiosity is stimulated, a child will concentrate on the description of events and increased interest in following the story. Greater cognitive effort leads to more appropriate judgements and a deeper understanding of the text.

Extrinsic motivation also encourages children to read, but through external demands and values. Some cases of extrinsic motivation may be counterproductive to text comprehension, as the reader pays only limited attention to aspects of the text, resulting in ineffective learning strategies and inaccurate inferences. Too much extrinsic motivation may negatively affect reading for enjoyment, while self-driven intrinsic motivation increases comprehension, as well as the amount children will read for personal enjoyment.

Summary

Reading is a process that our brains never evolved to do. To achieve reading success, we must develop two circuits, a dorsal circuit involved in grapheme-to-phoneme conversion and a ventral circuit involved in whole word access to pronunciation and meaning. The stages of reading involve a logographic stage where words are first recognised as objects, a phonological stage where the dorsal circuit is taught letter-sound relationships and an orthographic stage where dorsal and ventral circuits work fluently together.

Instruction in reading requires a solid foundation of language, both vocabulary and phonemic awareness. Initial instruction uses synthetic phonics that builds on itself in a progressive way. Here, letters are introduced and used with previously learnt letters to build words and read decodeable texts.

Many of the words in English are irregular and some will require direct learning so that they are available during reading and for writing. As the dorsal reading circuit develops an understanding for all the letter-sound correspondences, the reading brain becomes a self-teaching machine where new words can quickly be decoded and then added to the letterbox for quick access via the ventral circuit the next time the word is read. To gain fluency requires a considerable amount of contextual reading, where both circuits are working together and meaning is the final outcome.

4

The Spelling Brain

Spelling is the cognitive process of transcribing language into alphabetic letters. There are a number of spelling patterns in English that are standardised and must be learnt. Children will have a head start in spelling after learning phonics as an instructional method in reading. Spelling involves recognising common patterns, generalisations and some common rules.

The Neural Process of Spelling

Spelling is a process that involves both the dorsal and ventral circuits of the left brain. However for spelling, signals are heading down the reading circuits in the reverse direction.[20] While reading is processed from the letterbox in the back of the brain to the language systems in the front of the brain, spelling works from the front of the brain to the back of the brain (sound to visual).

The output of spelling is letter sequences, whereas the output of reading is pronunciations. Spelling begins with a word pronunciation in the front of the brain that accesses the corresponding word form (or letter sequence) in the letterbox at the back of the brain. This involves a directionality change in the ventral circuit.

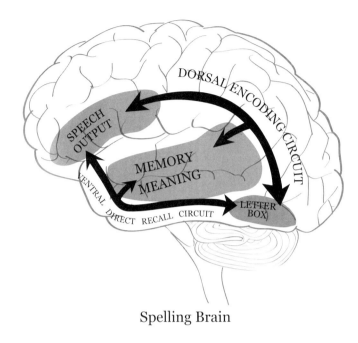

Spelling Brain

Figure 4.1 The Spelling Brain
The Spelling Brain engages the same circuits of the Reading Brain but in the reverse direction. The dorsal spelling circuit involves working from a word's pronunciation, to it's sounds, to the corresponding letters. The ventral circuit involves direct recall from a word's pronunciation to it's visual form.

Ventral 'Direct Recall' Circuit

When you imagine the written word, you are activating the letter box in the back of the brain. The letterbox provides a word's whole shape form for direct recall during spelling. The brain does not contain a different letterbox for reading and spelling. Rather each skill draws on the brain's letterbox, but with different inputs and outputs (directionality). Having one letterbox that connects the visual properties of words explains why reading and spelling abilities are so closely related. Brain imaging reports co-activation for reading and spelling in the letterbox of the ventral circuit, supporting the observation that there is shared brain activity in reading and spelling during whole word retrieval.

Sight vocabulary is quickly developed in the brain's letterbox through repeated exposure to new words during reading and writing. The letterbox not only provides rapid access to the correct word pronunciation during reading, it gives a visual image of the whole word form that can be used during spelling. These word representations will begin to weaken if they are not repeatedly reinforced during reading and spelling. Words that are used less frequently are the hardest to read and spell. Reading can become slower when switching from a favourite novel to a specific non-fiction topic. This also occurs with spelling. When trying to spell a word that is not seen or used often, it is likely that the letterbox only has a weak representation of this word with a low activation threshold, so it will be difficult to spell correctly. Representations in the letterbox are very much 'use it or lose it.'

Acquiring the spelling patterns of high frequency words saves emergent learners considerable time and energy as these words make up over half the words that are read and spelt. High frequency words are familiar from reading and already have representations in the brain's letterbox. Access to a word's form can be developed from its pronunciation. Direct recall provides perfect spellings when words have been correctly memorised. After a word has been memorised it is no longer considered just a group of letters, but a whole word form that has a pronunciation, meaning and spelling.

Dorsal 'Encoding' Circuit

Often spelling is not as simple as accessing a whole word shape. The letterbox cannot always provide all the words the brain wants to spell. Sometimes when trying to recall a word's spelling, the letterbox provides no answer. In fact, when first learning to spell, there will be very few words that can be accessed directly. If a spelling cannot be accessed directly from the letterbox, the brain's dorsal 'encoding' circuit can be used to produce the most likely spelling. Whereas the brain's ventral 'direct recall' circuit provides access to properties of whole word forms, the brain's dorsal 'encoding' circuit specialises in producing the letter/sound relationships that make up words.

The brain sometimes needs to rely on the dorsal circuit to decode a new word during reading. Spelling words that are not known also engages this dorsal circuit, but in the reverse direction. The computation behind spelling unknown words is encoding, where sounds are segmented from the word's pronunciation in the front of the brain and mapped onto individual letter patterns with the help of the dorsal circuit. Encoding produces the most likely spelling based on units of sound within the word. Encoding can be referred to as phoneme-to-grapheme conversion as it involves taking a unit of sound (phoneme) and mapping it onto a letter pattern (grapheme).

If the ventral 'direct recall' circuit can learn to spell through repeated exposure, what is the purpose of encoding? Encoding is used when a word's whole shape cannot be accessed, but a 'best guess' spelling is required. During written expression, by quickly producing a possible spelling for an unknown word, writing can continue, ensuring that meaning is not lost. The encoded spelling can later be checked in a dictionary. In a spelling test, the most likely spelling is attempted.

However encoding will not always produce the right spelling. The rules of decoding are more likely to produce a correct pronunciation during reading than the rules of encoding during spelling. This is because the 44 sounds of English are represented by over around 230 different graphemes. In comparison, Italian has 25 phonemes and 33 graphemes, making the whole process of encoding and decoding far simpler.

English Orthography

Why does encoding sometimes fail to produce the correct spelling? The English spelling system has low transparency as individual letters can be pronounced in multiple ways and there are a number of exception words. Inconsistencies observed in English spellings can be explained historically. English orthography evolved through a systematic layering of alphabet, patterns and meaning.

Old English existed between 500 and 1000 AD. Unlike today's English, the orthography of Old English showed remarkable consistency, or transparency, in letter/sound relationships. However, the Norman conquest of 1066 AD led to an overlay of French onto Old English by the ruling class. Any new vocabulary during this period followed French orthographic patterns and some of the words in Old English were changed to become consistent with the French structures. The Renaissance period during the 16th Century saw a large-scale borrowing of new vocabulary as the educated rediscovered classical Greek and Roman knowledge and culture. Greek and Latin words bought a morphemic (meaning) layer to English orthography and accommodated an explosion in learning.

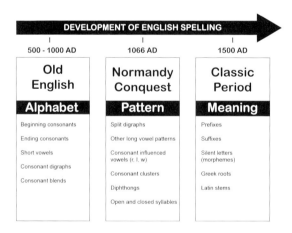

Figure 4.2 Development of English Spelling

The history of the English language explains how spelling has evolved. Similar to the historical progression of spelling, children follow their own developmental progression as the move from the alphabet to pattern to meaning relationships (Invernizzi and Hayes, 2004).

The history of orthographic structures provides different frequency-based tiers. Old English gives us most of our high frequency words such as prepositions, pronouns, conjunctions and auxiliary verbs (such as had, was, does). Many of our less frequent words were introduced during the Norman period (such as royal, guard, conquer). Finally, the classical period introduced low frequency words with Latin and Greek origins (such as auditorium, philosophy, spectator).

Figure 4.3 Transparency Across European Languages
Research into reading acquisition across European languages reveals some interesting results. Children in countries with transparent languages (languages that follow simple letter to sound correspondences) read accurately in the first year of school. However, children in other countries with more opaque languages (languages that have complex letter to sound rules) show difficulties in reading both real words and nonsense words in their first year of school - as represented by a higher error rate. In particular, England showed the poorest performance, where children could only read one out of three words presented (see Seymore, Aro & Erskine, 2003).

Teaching the Spelling Brain

Teaching the spelling brain involves a directionality shift for the dorsal and ventral reading circuits. Dorsal 'encoding' instruction involves teaching the relationships between the 44 sounds of English and how they map onto 230 graphemes. There are also a number of spelling conventions that can be taught which make this process easier.

As discussed, a number of words in English follow unusual spelling conventions based on the opaqueness of the English language and the history of orthography. For these cases, words may need to be learnt by rote in the ventral 'direct recall' circuit. Children's growing understanding of why words are spelt in a particular way is valuable only if they go on to apply it in their independent writing. Children should be able to spell an ever increasing number of words accurately and to check and correct their own work.

Teaching the Dorsal 'Encoding' Spelling Circuit

When children are writing, they need quick access to written word forms so that they can get their ideas down without interrupting their train of thought. As long as children follow the rules of encoding during writing, they will produce words that are phonologically accurate, that is, words that can be decoded to produce the correct pronunciation, even if they are spelt incorrectly. By using invented spellings, children can later check words they are unsure of in the dictionary to see how they are spelt.

Children should be encouraged to underline invented spellings if they don't look right, so that they can be checked later during editing. These words can also be added to individual spelling logs, provided the child's approximation is relatively close to the word being attempted. Invented spellings are useful during both child and teacher proof reading, as the story can be followed without having to guess the meaning behind a random misspelling. Research shows that children who use invented spellings write longer stories with more expressive vocabulary and make greater use of more complex grammatical structures. Thus encoding, which is a subcomponent of spelling, is also an important component of writing.

Spelling Conventions

Children will benefit from acquiring more word specific knowledge in the form of spelling conventions. They still need to segment words into phonemes to spell them, but they also learn that good spelling involves, where necessary, choosing the right grapheme from several possibilities.

The position of a phoneme may rule out certain graphemes when spelling. Some phonemes have different spellings at the end of words compared to within the word. For example, ai and oi do not occur at the end of words, whereas ay and oy do.

The relationship with a vowel to its neighbouring consonant can also change the phoneme sound. For example, the short 'a' when following 'w' makes the /o/ sound as in was, wallet, want, watch, wander. This is sometimes referred to as the w special and extends to cases where the /w/ sound comes from qu as in quarrel, quantity, squad, squash. When a /ur/ sound follows the letter 'w' it usually is spelt 'or', for example word, worm, work, worship, worth. The exception to this rule is 'were'. An /or/ sound before an /l/ sound is frequently spelled with the letter /a/, for example all, ball, call, always.

There are also positioning rules for consonants at the end of words. English words do not end in the letter v unless they are abbreviations (e.g. rev). If a word ends in a /v/ sound, e must be added after the v in the spelling, for example give, have, live, love, above. This may be confusing as it suggests the vowels should make their 'long' sounds (as in alive, save and stove). There are few words in this short vowel category (give/have). As most are high-frequency they should be quickly learnt.[21]

Figure 4.4 Spelling Game
The game Spelligator teaches letter patterns by stacking tiles on a toy alligator. Children compete to see who can build the tallest spelligator (the most number of words) and win the game. The game is also rich in phonemic awareness as it involves breaking words into sounds and adding sounds to make new words.

Adding Suffixes

Most children will have taken suffixes in their stride during reading, but for spelling purposes suffixes need more systematic teaching. Important teaching points are both the suffixes themselves and how the spelling of base words may have to change slightly when suffixes are added. Some grammatical awareness is also helpful here. Just knowing that the regular past tense ending is spelt −ed is not enough. Children also need to be aware that the word they are trying to spell is a past tense word. Without this awareness they may for example try to spell hopped as hopt, played as plaid, grabbed as grabd and started as startid – perfectly accurate phonemically, but incorrect. Conversely, once they have understood that the –ed ending can sometimes sound like /t/, they may try to spell soft as soffed, unless they realise that this is not the past tense of a verb.

Generally, -s as a suffix is simply added to the base word. The suffix –es is added after words ending in s, ss, ch, sh, z and zz, and when y is replaced with an i (baby – babies). The –es creates an extra syllable which is easy to hear in words such as buses, passes, benches, catches, rushes. Words such as knife, leaf, and loaf become knives, leaves, and loaves and again the change in spelling is obvious from the change in the pronunciation of these words.

Other suffixes include –ing, -ed, -ful, -er, -est, -ly, -ment, -ness, and –y. Often, they can be added to base words without affecting the spelling of the base word. Adding a suffix may sometimes mean, however, that the last letter of the base word needs to be dropped, changed or doubled.

There are three types of base words that need their last letters changed. The first is base words ending in an –e which is part of the split digraph (e.g. hope, safe, use). Here, drop the e if the suffix begins with a vowel (e.g. hope – hoping), but keep the e if the suffix begins with a consonant (e.g. hope – hopeful). The second is base words ending in –y proceeded by a consonant (e.g. happy, baby, carry). Here, change a y to an i before adding suffixes (happy + er = happier) except for suffixes beginning with i (baby + ish = babyish). Finally, base words ending in a single consonant letter preceded by a single vowel letter (e.g. hop, red, run). Here, double the final consonant (e.g. run – running).

Figure 4.5 Tri-Blocks
Tri-blocks are an intelligent spelling system that allow children to build a complete range of letter sound patterns based on these unique interlocking blocks. At the simple level, children can practise building CVC (consonant vowel consonant) words. The blocks also rotate for practising the manipulation of

sounds. At a higher level, children can make split digraph words (containing the magic e), multi-syllabic words (with the innovative syllable connector block) and finally add suffixes (making use of specific rule such as change the y to an i and adding es or doubling the n (on a CVC word) when adding -ing.

Teaching the Ventral 'Direct Recall' Circuit

As there are more graphemes than phonemes in English, it is possible to encode words in multiple ways leading to potential misspellings. In some cases, word-specific spellings (e.g. sea/see; goal/pole/bowl/soul; zoo/clue/flew/you) simply have to be learned. It is important to devote time to common words with rare or irregular spellings (e.g. they, there, said) as the amount of writing children do increases. Without correction they may practise incorrect spellings that are later difficult to put right.

Homophones

Homophones are words that sound the same but have different meanings, such as rose (the flower) and rose (to lift up). Homophones can also be spelt differently but make the same sound. These are called hetrographic homophones, such as to, two and too. Confusions are common between their and there and can persist unless appropriate teaching is given. 'There' is related in meaning and spelling to here and where – all are concerned with place. 'Their' is related in meaning (plural person) and spelling to they and them.

To avoid confusing children, experience shows that it is advisable not to teach these two similar sounding words 'there' and 'their' at the same time but to secure the understanding of one of them before teaching the other.

Silent Letters

Silent letters are letters in words that do not contribute to the pronunciation. They make it difficult to read and spell a word. Spellers must learn that the silent letter or letters are part of the standard spelling of these words and learn not to pronounce them when reading.

Contractions

A contraction consists of two words that are combined to form one word. Sometimes known as elisions, such as I'm, let's and can't are usually easy to spell, but children need to know where to put the apostrophe. They should be taught that it marks the place where letters are omitted.

Irregular Tenses

Before teaching children to spell in the past tense form of verbs, it is important that they gain an understanding of the meaning of 'tense'. Since many common verbs have irregular past tenses (e.g. go – went, come – came, say – said) it is often easier to teach the concept of past tense from the spelling of past tense forms. Games using the words yesterday and today can reinforce the different meanings of verb tenses.

Spelling Log

Children can have a spelling log to record the particular spellings they need to focus on in their work. It gives children an opportunity to identify specific words they need to continue to work on. These could be words exemplifying a particular pattern or high frequency words. These words can be put into children's logs with tips on how to remember the spelling.

Words specific to the individual child that come up in independent writing and frequently trip them up should be added to the log. Target words can be identified during the proofreading process. Children can be involved in devising strategies for learning them and for monitoring how well they are doing. Children should have no more than five target words at a time. They can look for evidence of correct spellings in their independent writing and remove a word from the list once it has been spelt correctly five times in a row.

Summary

Spelling is a process of transcribing the correct letters in the correct order for spoken words. The two dorsal and ventral reading circuits are used in the reverse direction for spelling words. A dorsal 'encoding' circuit is used for mapping phoneme sounds onto possible grapheme correspondences.

Encoding does not always produce the correct spelling, but it will produce a phonologically accurate spelling that is useful in writing (refer to as an invented spelling). Often, the words of English contain irregular orthographic patterns. The ventral 'direct recall' circuit is used to access the visual whole-word form. Sometimes, words in English need to be learnt by rote so that they are freely available for the ventral 'direct recall' circuit.

5

The Writing Brain

Writing is a distinctly human activity. It involves transcribing language through the creation of symbols to represent words. Writing becomes an effective method of recording thoughts, events and ideas, as it is not reliant on human memory. Handwriting is a person's unique style of writing with a pencil or pen and is taught alongside reading and spelling.

Mirror Writing

It is not unusual for children to spontaneously write backwards when they are first learning to write. This phenomenon appears to occur across all languages. Another commonly observed practice is confusion between b and d both in reading and writing when children begin to develop literacy skills. Although these reversals are often referred to as soft signs of dyslexia, letter reversals are common in all early writers until the brain works out the correct orientations. Reversals should no longer continue (beyond the ages of seven to ten) once children have acquired the correct orientations.

Neurological theories have attempted to explain why the letters b and d are so commonly confused.[22] Letters are projected into the left or right visual systems (in the back of the brain) depending on the visual field where the letter is seen. If the letter is left of the mid line it will project to the right brain and if it is right of the mid line it will project to the left brain. Luckily, our corpus callosum (the nerve bundle that links the two hemispheres) shares the information with the other side so that both sides of our brain can see what is going on.

Visual information in the right brain is a mirror reflection of visual information in the left brain, but as the information moves across to the left hemisphere it flips on itself with a left-right inversion (like a glove or mirror image). The corpus callosum is wired to do this for us, so there no disturbance or confusion in our visual field. A left profile of a tiger in the left brain is a right profile of a tiger in the right brain. Having both profiles of a tiger means we can recognise danger quickly. However, because of this evolutionary process, a 'b' in the left brain will actually represent itself as a 'd' in the right brain.

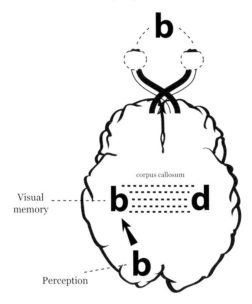

Figure 5.1 B and D Reversals
When we see a letter it can enter either the left or right hemisphere (according to the visual field where the letter is recognised). If it arrives in the right brain, it is flipped (by the corpus callosum) as it makes it's way across to the left brain. In doing so a 'b' can be confused as a 'd'. The brain needs to supress it's process of flipping the letter to ensure that b's and d's are read correctly (Corballis et al., 1985).

The problem for children doesn't happen when they see the letter but when they try to memorise it. If they first learn the letter b in their left brain (and link it to the name bee), when they see the letter 'd' the following day in their right brain they will automatically map it across to their left hemisphere and read it as a 'b'. As the letters 'b and d' are the same object viewed from different angles our evolutionary brain wants to recognise it quickly. However, this doesn't help us with the task of recognising letters. We need to learn to suppress the right hemispheres recognition of a 'b' as a 'd'.

There are two different circuits involved in visual processing – a dorsal stream and a ventral stream. The dorsal stream (or the 'what' stream) is a perceptual stream providing detailed information of the visual world and is involved with object recognition and form representation. It includes the letterbox in its pathway. The dorsal stream (or the 'where' stream) is an action stream that is involved in the guidance of movements. It recognises where objects are in space.

The 'where' stream is capable from telling right from left as this is important in movement control. The 'where' stream can adapt our movement to object orientation (tiger on our left – run right) whereas the 'what' stream tells us what the object is (tiger – alert, alert!). Research into the 'where' stream shows it contains multiple circuits that control hand movement, eye movement, and the understanding of an object in space.[23]

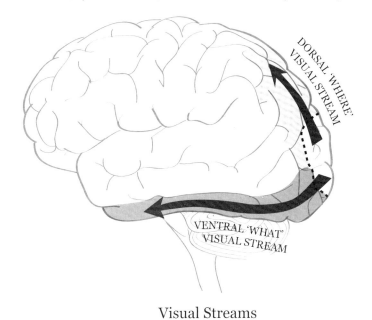

Visual Streams

Figure 5. 2 Visual Steams
The visual system at the back of the brain also separates information into two circuits. A dorsal visual stream that is involved with processing an object in space (where pathway) and a ventral visual stream that is involved with object recognition (what pathway).

It is believed that this dorsal stream (or where stream) plays an important role in early reading and writing as it enables the brain to unlearn the mirror-image generalisations that are pre-programmed by evolution. The 'where' stream forces the letterbox to break its symmetry and not to confuse b and d as views of the same object. Rather they must be learnt as individual letters in their own right with distinct neural populations.

Within the 'what stream', neighbouring cortical regions involved in object and face recognition continue to generalise left-right distinctions. However, the letterbox ceases to confuse mirror images and makes a break from symmetry for the written characters it represents. When children write letters, they are associating them with a distinct gesture or movement. By learning each letter as a two dimensional form, each letter is no longer susceptible to spatial rotation. It is no longer the same object from a different view point, but a fixed two dimensional object of the letter b.

There are a number of lesion studies that support this neurological model of visual representations. Patients with damage to the dorsal stream (lesions to the parietal lobe) can often lose the ability to tell the difference between left and right. They can also lose the ability to recognise mirrored objects. Interestingly, patients with hemiplegia (inability to use one side of their body) often write in mirror writing when using their non-dominant (but still functional) left hands. This appears specific to writing as they cannot mirror read the words they have written.

Brain Research on Writing

Research on the brain structures involved in handwriting is limited and focuses primarily on the processes behind spelling and writing (not creative writing or planning a story). There are limitations on performing brain-imaging studies of the handwriting processes as writing requires gross arm movements within the scanner which may involve head movements and result in image artefacts. Unfortunately, there are only a limited number of brain-imaging studies (so far) to investigate the writing brain.

A Circuit for Handwriting

Letter production involves assigning each letter a written form. A writing circuit runs from a parietal region in the back of the brain (involved with graphical images of letters) forward to a frontal region (that contains letter-motor plans). This circuit appears to be universal across different languages and writing systems.

Exner's area in the frontal lobe is believed to be the final common pathway where linguistic impulses receive their motor pattern for the purpose of writing. Hand movements specific to writing are controlled by this area including uppercase / lowercase, cursive versus printing and the individual differences that make each person's handwriting unique.

Typing also significantly activates this region. This area is adjacent to the frontal expressive speech area (Broca's) and other areas controlling the movement of the hand and fine finger control.

Exner's area is very dependent on the speech area and there are extensive interconnections between the two. Direct cortical stimulation of Exner's area disrupts writing, but does not disrupt hand movement itself. Damage to Exner's area through stroke results in disturbances in the motor aspects of writing, where handwriting becomes laboured, uncoordinated and takes a very sloppy appearance. Cursive handwriting can be more affected than print as it requires further fine motor control. After lesion, there may also be disturbances in letter selection where the wrong letters are chosen or abnormally sequenced.

The other area involved in writing is the inferior parietal lobe, an area considered to be involved in spatial and motor planning. The inferior parietal lobe processes visual-auditory motor impulses (most likely with the help of Wernicke's area in the temporal lobe) and assists in programming sensory-motor movements through space. These impulses are mapped forward to Exner's area.[24] When subjects imagine they are writing by hand, this parietal area is shown to activate.

Damage to the inferior parietal lobe by stroke also results in placing letters in the wrong order or sequence, presumably because the area involved in organising visual-letter formation (inferior parietal lobe) is no longer connected to the area controlling hand movement (Exner's Area). Damage to the inferior parietal lobe can also result in distortions and inversions in letter formations.

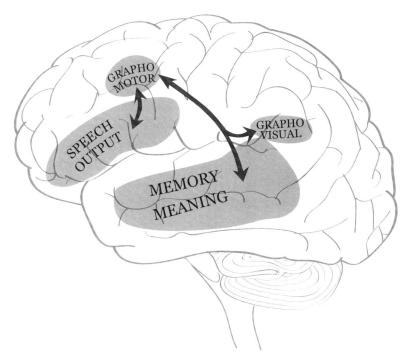

Handwriting Brain

Figure 5. 3 The Handwriting Brain
Handwriting involves fine motor movement in the front of the brain, linked to visual-spatial processing in parietal and temporal regions of the brain.

This circuit for handwriting (involving frontal and parietal areas) plays an important role in orthographic working memory. While reading and spelling are reverse processes, spelling places a higher demand on working memory as the output is the sequencing of letters (as opposed to accessing the pronunciation).

As discussed previously, words of up to seven letters can be read at the same speed because the letters are processed by the lower circuit in parallel. This is not the same in spelling. Spelling words containing three phonemes (such as 'sew') can be spelt faster than matched words with three phonemes but with many more graphemes (such as 'through'). This word length effect of spelling on working memory is shown to light up the handwriting circuit during brain imaging experiments.[25] Interestingly, stroke patients with damage to regions on the writing circuit also show working memory deficits for spelling.

Teaching the Writing Brain

Letters made of sandpaper allow children to feel the shape of a letter and to see the shape it makes. By placing a piece of paper over a sandpaper letter, children can trace the shape for themselves before writing skills have been properly developed. Sandpaper letters allow children to feel the shape of letters, see the shape of letters and trace the shape of letters. Activities with sandpaper letters support the multi-sensory approach, bringing together gestures, touch, vision and a sense of space.

Figure 5.4 Sandpaper Letters
Sandpaper letters are a Montessori approach for teaching letter shapes and formations. By touching the sandpaper children can feel the shape of the letter.

As children progress in handwriting, the development of a fluent joined style is an important part of learning to spell and the teaching of spelling and handwriting can be closely linked. Children can practice joining each digraph as one unit as they learn the basic joins of handwriting. This can develop into practising letter strings and complete words linked to the phonics progression or a spelling rule. High-frequency words can be demonstrated and practised as joined units (e.g. the, was, said). Children need to see their target spelling words written in joined script as frequently as possible. They can practice writing these words in dictations and at home using joined script.

Proof Reading

Handwriting is guided by visual feedback as the writer observes the appearance of the letters and words that he or she is writing. Once the letters of a word have been selected, sequenced and written down, the brain needs to self-check, to make sure the spelling is correct. The brain uses the ventral reading circuit to access the word from the letterbox and map it forward to the pronunciation. If the word is not recognised, it is not stored in the brain's letterbox and must be checked using a dictionary or an editing card. If the word is recognised, then it has been accessed in the letterbox and its spelling is confirmed.

Children need to be taught how to proofread their work as part of the writing process. Editing for spelling should take place after the writer is satisfied with all other elements of the writing. It is important that teachers model the proofreading process in shared writing. Here, the teacher reads through the work as the children follow, underlining the part of the word and explaining why it looks wrong. The children are encouraged to provide an alternative spelling, and to ask themselves whether it looks right.

Finally, the children should check from another source (such as words around the room, spelling log or dictionary) and then write the correct spelling. This process is repeated until all the target words are corrected. Teachers can monitor patterns in these errors and consider strategies that might help the children avoid the same errors in the future. After shared writing, these proofreading strategies are transferred into guided writing and independent writing.

Children should be taught to use a dictionary to check their spelling. The repeated singing of the alphabet song when younger should have familiarised them with alphabetical order. Their first dictionary practice should be with words starting with different letters, but once they are competent with this, they can learn to look at second (and then subsequent letters when necessary), learning for example that words starting with sc- come before words starting sl- and st-, and words starting fam- come before words starting fas- and fat-.

Knowledge of the different ways of spelling phonemes is also relevant in dictionary use. For example, a child who tries to look up 'believe' under belee- needs to be reminded to look under other possible spellings of the /ee/ sound. Once children find the correct spelling of a word, they should be encouraged to memorise it.

When using a spell checker, unless a first attempt at spelling a word is logical and reasonably close to the target, the suggested words may be quite different from the one required. Children need to be taught not just to accept these suggestions but to sound them out carefully. This becomes a 'double-check' as to whether the pronunciation matches the words that they are trying to spell.

Modelling Writing

Just as reading instruction involves a balance of reading to, with and by children, writing instruction involves a balance of writing to, with and by children. Shared writing is used to demonstrate the links between spoken and written text, where teachers use the children's ideas to construct the story. Children can take part in planning, discussing and revising the writing.

Shared writing can be used to introduce new genres to the class such as letter writing and poetry. Non-fictional texts, such as recollection, instruction, report, explanation and discussion can also be introduced through this medium. Guided writing moves from teacher demonstration to teacher modelling, where the teacher and the children plan the writing together, but the children then construct their own pieces.

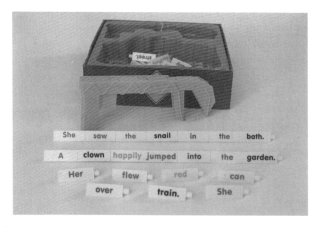

Figure 5.5 Sentence Building Game
Construct A Sentence is a sentence building game that teaches parts of speech as well as sentence formation. Children are encouraged to take a block with the toy crane. Each block contains a colour-coded word that can be linked together to make a sentence. Words can also be rotated within the sentence to change the meaning of the sentence.

Marking provides the opportunity to see how well individual children understand and apply what has been taught and should always relate to the specific focus of teaching. By analysing children's errors, teachers can investigate the strategies that children are using. For example, a child using jumpt instead of jumped is using phonological knowledge but does not yet understand about adding –ed to verbs in the past tense.

Teachers must set expectations for independent spelling in terms of simple targets that will apply to all the writing children do. These targets would generally be differentiated for groups, but it may be appropriate to target specific 'problem' words for an individual (e.g. I expect to spell these words correctly in all my writing: said, they). Teachers should not however be side-tracked by spelling errors when working with children on their writing. If a teacher's first comments on a child's writing are concerned with spelling or handwriting then the child will start to think that these things are the most valued in writing. Moreover, both reading and writing are principally meaning driven processes. The writer has to construct meaning for the intended reader. Just as good readers re-read when they lose meaning, good writers must re-read and re-write when meaning is lost.

Conferencing during guided writing is used as a form of direct scaffolding where a teacher works one-on-one with a child to help them with their story. For example, the meaning of a story might be lost because a child has omitted an introductory sentence to put a story into context. By discussing this with the child, an introductory sentence can be created to enhance the story. In the same way, a better word can be introduced to describe something. This learning affects children's future written expression, when scaffolding is no longer needed.

The final edited product can be prepared on a word processor and printed so the child has a copy of the published version. The published story is then available for a broader audience to read and enjoy, such as other children, teachers and parents. The more children engage in conferencing, revising and publishing, the better their reading, spelling and writing skills will become. As children master the skill of writing they can interchange between the roles of storyteller and story reader and develop self-conferencing.

Technology and Writing

As children get older, they can embrace written communication with friends through instant messaging, e-mails, social networking, and fast paced text messaging on their phones. Some parents and teachers worry that this informal e-communication might be damaging children's writing skills with relaxed punctuation, grammar, and a preference for abbreviations and acronyms.

Most children understand that electronic communication is not 'real writing' and fits into the same category as phone calls and face to face speaking. However, informal writing may bleed into school work, more commonly in note taking, but occasionally in formal written assignments. In some teenagers it may also infiltrate spoken language, such as the use of LOL or OMG. Children need to understand the differences between informal writing (where grammar and spelling are sometimes sacrificed for concision and speed) and formal writing (where conventions must be followed) and learn not to mix the two.

In today's world children are often using computers for their composition and writing. Some children find that computers offer them advantages in speed and neatness. Others feel it is easier to structure their ideas and unleash their creativity when writing by hand. Often, these decisions are not theirs to make as the use of hand or computer is decided by the school or teacher.

For a number of children, the ability to edit and revise text is one of the major advantages of a computer. Computers also offer spell checking and predictive spellings. This technology will help children, but should not replace proofreading as some words, such as homophones (for example there and their), might not be picked up if spelt incorrectly.

Children are also using the internet as their primary method for researching assignments. Across the internet they may become aware of the minor differences between British and American English and learn to choose and be consistent with the correction conventions for the audience they are writing for. Children also need to question the accuracy of information when using the internet for research.

Summary

Writing is the process of transcribing language into a written form that contains meaning and can be accessed by others. Mirror reversals are often observed when children first learn to write and this can be explained by how the left and right brain are wired. As children learn to master handwriting (and reading) they will suppress the brains natural tendency to mirror flip letters and no longer make left/right confusions. Unfortunately there has been little brain research into writing and the brain. Lesion studies along with a handful of brain-imaging studies describe a writing circuit that involves Exner's Area in the front of the brain for grapho-motor store and parietal areas for spatial information on letters. Teaching handwriting should be a multi-sensory experience and move towards cursive joined script that is integrated with reading, phonics or spelling instruction. Children should be encouraged to write for pleasure. Just like reading, writing (and proofreading) can be taught at shared, guided and independent levels.

6

The Mathematical Brain

Young children are presented with numbers everywhere in their everyday environment. Mathematics ability gives them the skills they need to make sense in the world they live in. The mathematical brain is present in infants and is believed to be an evolutionary sense that is hard wired into the brain. Primary numeric abilities include subitising, counting, ordinality and arithmetic.

Mathematical Processes

Subitising is our ability to see a number of objects and to estimate the number without actually counting each object.[26] For example, when we see four dots on a die we instantly know we have rolled a four without having to count the four dots. The brain can subitise up to five items rapidly and accurately. Beyond five it is less accurate and confident. It also takes the brain longer to process – about 300 msecs for each additional item added. At this stage we are counting beyond the subitised number.

Neuropsychology points to different mechanisms behind subitising and counting. Subitising is considered a parallel process, as the cost of an additional item is only 50 msecs, so processes are happening at the same time to subitise or predict the number. For counting, the time cost of 300 msecs suggests a more serial process where the brain must work through each item individually to compute the total number in a set.

Subitising is an innate ability and observable in humans from birth. It has evolutionary importance as it lets us know quickly how many predators are in front of us.

Ordinality concerns the orders that number come in. Just like in reading we understand the order of the alphabet from A – Z, with numbers we need to know the order of numbers from 1-10 and beyond. Once we understand this concept we can also understand the concepts of more than or less than along this ordinal line. Finally, basic arithmetic involves combining and decreasing quantities of small sets. This is the underlying concept behind addition and subtraction.

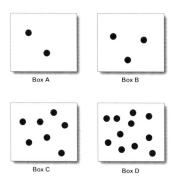

Figure 6.1 Subitising

Subitising involves looking at the dots quickly to process the number. For up to 5 objects, items or dots, our brain's can subitise and provide the number very quickly. Beyond this we need to manually count to get an accurate answer.

Ironically, just as English is not well suited for phonology in reading, it is also not well suited for corresponding to the base – 10 ordinal structure of the Arabic numbering system. For example, English has special words between 10 and 20 (eleven, twelve, thirteen...), names for decades (twenty, thirty, forty...) and a gap for names between thousand and million.

Chinese on the other hand has the benefit of number names in base ten which are entirely regular. So Chinese children can count to ten the normal way and then continue ten-one, ten-two, ten-three (instead of eleven, twelve, thirteen...). When they reach the twenties they can count: two-ten-one, two-ten-two, two-ten-three and so on. It has been argued that this language advantage allows Asian students to outperform western students based on speed and accuracy in mathematical calculations.

The Neural Process of Mathematics

Early brain research on mathematics investigated stroke patients who have lost the ability to calculate. A common finding is that damage to the parietal lobe results in difficulty performing mathematical operations. Brain-imaging converges with lesion studies to show that in normal subjects there is an area within the parietal lobe that lights up during mathematical processing. This region activates in both the left and right side of the brain and shows different activations patterns depending on the mathematical operation being solved (addition, subtraction, multiplication, division).

The left-right lateralization of this number module may be contingent on the level of language involvement. It is believed that the left region is connected to the linguistic code allowing the language system to access quantity information.

For tasks not requiring language such as number comparison, the right parietal region shows stronger activation, perhaps because there is no linguistic translation required. The number sense in the parietal lobe is also involved in number approximation or estimation. Again these processes are outside of linguistic processing and tie closer to visual-spatial operations. Indeed, the location of the number sense in the parietal lobe sits close to the processing centres for mental rotation and hand movement – a link between finger (digit) counting and number processing.

The Dorsal 'Quantitative' Circuit

An understanding of the number sense in the parietal lobe is a first step towards developing a cognitive neuro-anatomical model of number processing. Number sense is located on a dorsal circuit that can encode quantity representations and manipulate these representations based on mathematical operations. Manipulations are performed on these internal quantities and their answers are fed back to the language system for oral or written output. It is in the dorsal 'mathematical' circuit where the brains mental number line is stored. The brain can use this number line for addition and subtraction manipulation when adding or subtracting along the line.

The Ventral 'Memorised Calculation' Circuit

While the dorsal 'quantitative' circuit is bilaterally represented (on both left and right sides), the ventral 'memorised calculation' circuit is on the left side and links directly into language systems. The ventral 'memorised calculation' circuit also accesses the visual number form from a Numberbox (that sits before the letterbox on the ventral visual stream). From the Numberbox a mathematical problem is analysed (for example 2 + 2) and trans-coded into language (two plus two).

As the ventral circuit projects forward to trans-code the equation into language, the completion of the equation is provided using rote verbal memory (two plus two is four). The sub-processing behind the ventral 'memorised calculation' circuit is visual identification, visual-verbal trans-coding and verbal sequence completion. This becomes the preferred circuit for processing over-learned calculations.[27] In many respects it is like using the ventral reading circuit to read $2 + 2$ as 'four'. The ventral 'memorised calculation' circuit is blind to the quantity representation it is reading and just produces the right answer.

The dorsal 'quantitative' circuit is also capable of processing the same equation by using its internal visual number line system, but as this requires more processing (than direct verbal recall) it will be more energy and time consuming. Thus, the ventral 'memorised calculation' circuit has an advantage for solving simple over-learned sums. Evidence of this effect comes from studies of bilingual students who when asked to calculate often report that they have to utter the numerals in the language they first learnt arithmetic in at school.

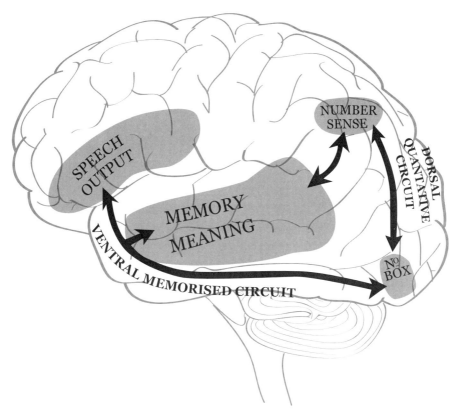

Mathematical Brain

Figure 6.2 The Mathematical Brain
The Mathematical Brain has two circuits for processing numbers. A ventral circuit can recognise number patterns and equations and project these forward to rote memory. A dorsal circuit is used for actually processing mathematical concepts and this occurs in the number sense area of the parietal lobe.

Dorsal vs Ventral 'Mathematical' Circuits

Addition and subtraction are reverse operations of each other. Addition involves adding further quantities to the set whereas subtraction involves taking quantities away. It would seem intuitive that each operation might involve the same circuit in the brain, such as decoding and encoding are reverse operations across the dorsal reading circuit. This is not the case.

Within early education children are encouraged to rote learn addition facts. They practise counting up from one. They commit time tables to memory. All of this learning has a strong language component as we chant the equation we are trying to learn.

However, while all this rote learning occurs for addition, it does not occur as often for subtraction. For example, we practise counting up from one, in ones (or in twos), but it is harder for us to count backwards from 50 in ones (or twos) because we don't practice this as often. Thus, addition and even more so multiplication, has a ventral 'memorised calculation' circuit advantage, whereas subtraction and division have a stronger dorsal 'quantitative' circuit advantage. This advantage is more distinct, the more common the addition or multiplication equation. More advanced addition or multiplication (such as $17 + 26$ or 8×9) is more likely to have a dorsal 'quantitative' circuit component as it is less likely available from verbal memory.[28]

The fact that we can separate out these circuits does not suggest that they work independently from each other, especially in normal students. For most calculations these circuits will be activating simultaneously and supporting each other to achieve the most accurate, efficient and fast solution – just like in reading. For example, the dorsal 'quantitative' circuit can use its magnitude interpretation of number to evaluate the plausibility of the answer produced from the ventral 'memorised calculation' circuit (as retrieved from verbal memory).

In adults, multiplication is solved mainly by the ventral circuit and division almost certainly requires a search through these tables in the ventral circuit. The ventral 'memorised calculation' circuit is also the preferred circuit in adults for addition however the dorsal circuit is still available and supportive in guiding verbal number production or arithmetic fact retrieval.

Subtraction, whilst more likely involves the dorsal 'quantitative' circuit, can draw on the ventral circuit to provide related addition facts such as $11 - 7 =$ by drawing on $4 + 7 = 11$ and the same is certainly true for division. Even for multiplication, different strategies are available which can involve both the ventral and dorsal mathematical circuits such as $9 \times 9 = (9 \times 10) - 9 = 81$ where 9×10 can be retrieved by the ventral circuit and $- 9$ by the dorsal circuit resulting in the answer 81. Thus, the normal operation of number processing will involve fast multi-directional interactions across the dorsal and ventral mathematical circuits.

Stroke patients with lesions to mathematical circuits are referred to as having acalculia. Studies into acalculia support this neuro-anatomical model of mathematics. Two types of acalculia have been observed, those with a more pure type who have problems comprehending numerical concepts and performing arithmetic calculations and others who showed problems with calculation due to memory difficulties. The subtype of acalculia involving damage to the dorsal 'quantitative' circuit is called quantitative acalculia. Subjects with quantitative acalculia have reported significantly more difficulties with subtraction than addition and multiplication.

Another subtype called surface acalculia report significantly more difficulties with multiplication than addition or subtraction, including simple problems (2 x 3 or 3 x 2). A noticeable clinical characteristic is slowness in calculation. For very simple addition tasks, both subtypes can perform well, presumably because such addition problems can be solved successfully by using either the dorsal or ventral mathematical circuits independently.

Teaching the Mathematical Brain

Counting becomes an important first step in the understanding of numbers. Different mathematical language will be introduced during learning to direct mathematical processes. The following proposed framework is structured around early instruction for teaching the dorsal and ventral mathematical circuits. The acquisition of number concepts is best supported by multi-sensory techniques.

Teaching the Dorsal 'Quantitative' Circuit

Teaching the dorsal 'quantitative' circuit will involve counting objects to determine how many are in a set. Visual mathematics is used to demonstrate patterns, order and groups. The dorsal 'mathematical' circuit houses the brain's internal number line.

By presenting numbers with an array of digits in an ordinal number line, students can visualise number patterns and perform number bisection tasks (which number falls between 5 and 7) independently of verbal working memory. Here, children can see the operations of addition and subtraction as movement along or backward across the number line.

The dorsal 'quantitative' circuit benefits from the use of manipulatives because of the multi-sensory opportunities. Manipulatives can be used to visually demonstrate greater or less than in number comparisons, addition and subtraction sequencing, number bisection, the four operations, fractions and place value.

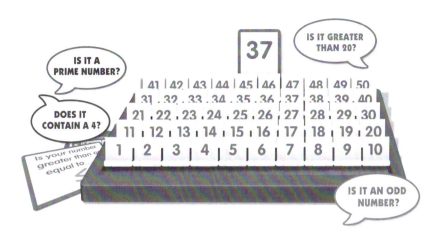

Figure 6. 3 Number Grid
Number grids are an effective way to teach number patterns and operations. What's My Number is a game that uses a number grid for working out an opponents number. Various cards are provided to help children ask questions regarding the properties of the number.

Teaching the Ventral 'Memorised Calculation' Circuit

Teaching the ventral circuit will involve understanding number words, numerals and the ability to say number names in order. Children will be encouraged to learn addition facts and multiplication by rote. Numeracy rhymes can be used to support the verbal memorization of number facts at the earlier stages. At a higher level, children will be provided with word equations and can transpose these into number equations for solving. Flash cards, mathematical raps, and mathematic nursery rhymes can be used to help build and reinforce the ventral 'memorised calculation' circuit, especially for those who have difficulty in rote verbalisation of mathematical facts.

Stages of Mathematics Instruction

Like reading, mathematics can be taught systematically, building on concepts previously taught. Stages of mathematics are introduced, each with increasing number complexity (i.e Stage 1: introduction of numbers; Stage 2: numbers 1-5; Stage 3: numbers 1-10; Stage 4: numbers 0-20; Stage 5: numbers 0-50; Stage 6: numbers 0-100). Across each stage, importance is given to recognising, using and memorising number patterns.

Learning mathematics involves children understanding patterns in number names, both the rhymes and rhythms in sounds and the common visual patterns. Memorisation becomes easier and recall more immediate as children begin to learn how the patterns are structured and how their underlying formation can be applied to new contexts. Teaching should involve practical, hands-on exploration and play.[29]

Stage 1: Introduction to Quantity

Stage 1 focuses on the development of children's early awareness of quantity and the use of the language of number. The following key vocabulary can be introduced to teach quantity: more, less, few, more than, less than, fewer, fewer than, number, one, many, lots, lots of, a few, a lot, order, count, pattern, same, next, one, two, three... How many? Which/what number...? What does this number tell us? Indoor and outdoor activities involving quantitative awareness are excellent for identifying number patterns and practicing key vocabulary.

Stage 2: Numbers 1-5

At Stage 2 children develop knowledge and use of the number sequence from one to five, recognition of the numerals 1 to 5, counting up to five objects and subitising (instantly recognising without counting) sets of one, two and three objects. The following key vocabulary can be used in instruction: number, order, count, after, one, two, three, four, five, forwards, backwards, straight, curved, What number comes next? How many..? What does the number look like?, least, fewer, amount, the same as. Number nursery rhymes can be used for teaching the counting sequence and these can be supported with actions and movements. Number names can be over-pronounced to help children learn these names accurately. Children should be encouraged to see the link between number word forms and numerals in a range of fonts including the written form. Explore visual and tactile opportunities to teach the shapes of numerals. Use 'thinking aloud' real life examples to demonstrate how counting helps with organization. Model counting strategies such as touching each object as you count it, move objects into groups and place objects in a line.

Stage 3: Numbers 1-10

The main focus in Stage 3 is number recognition from 1 to 10 in terms of sequencing and object counting. Key vocabulary at Stage 3 includes: number, order, count, one, two, three, four, five, six, seven, eight, nine, ten, forwards, backwards, next, before, straight, curved, What number comes next? How many...? What does the number look like?, more, less, few, more than, fewer, fewer than, amount, same as, How many altogether?

Children should be encouraged to chant the number sequence, both forward and backward, through number songs and rhymes. When counting through a sequence, pause the count and ask: What comes next? As children hear the numbers, show them the numbers on cards so they can see the shape of the numeral and the written form as well. Children can look for everyday opportunities to count groups of objects. Encourage children to count on their fingers and in their heads.

Counting can be modelled with movement of objects from one location to another or by placing objects in a line. Objects can be marked as they are counted by turning them over or by placing a counter top on them. Sets containing objects can be compared in terms of which number is bigger, smaller or the same.

Stage 4: Numbers 0 – 20

Stage 4 extends the range of numbers from 0 to 20. Children should be able to count up to ten objects in any arrangement. As children begin to partition and combine sets to remove objects from sets they will develop early stages of addition and subtraction. Key vocabulary at Stage 4 are: number, order, count, zero, eleven, twelve, thirteen, fourteen, fifteen, sixteen, seventeen, eighteen, nineteen, twenty, first, second, third, forwards, backwards, next, before, between, pattern, sequence, What number comes next? How many...?, total, more, less, more than, less than, fewer, fewer than, amount, one more, one less, estimate, guess, before, after, How many altogether?, How many left?

A wide range of starting points can be used to rehearse counting forwards and backwards. Introduce the word zero in daily language, for example when reading out telephone numbers. Provide number tracks and number lines for modelling the sequence of counting numbers, demonstrating before, after, between, and missing numbers. Explain how two digits are needed to form the numbers 10 to 20. Create opportunities for introducing ordinal language such as first, second, third in appropriate contexts.

Count objects by pointing or nodding at them in turn. Help children to understand that they can find one more or one less by counting on or back, rather than recounting the whole set. Explore the partitioning of numbers in different ways. For example, four can be partitioned into three and one, or two and two. Help children to notice the patterns in such sequences.

Stage 5: Numbers 0 – 50

By Stage 5, the number range which children can confidently use is extended to 50. Children can also start exploring different sequence of numbers when they count from zero in twos, fives and tens. Counting skills can be extended to enable them to estimate, count and compare sets of up to 20 objects. Addition and subtraction are further developed as children partition and combine sets and count on and back. Key vocabulary at Stage 5 include: number, order, count, pattern, zero, twenty-one, twenty-two…, twenty-nine, ten, twenty, thirty, forty, fifty, forwards, backwards, next, before, between, sequence, first, second, third, fourth, fifth… What number comes next? How many…? What order…?, estimate, about, more, less, most, least, more than, less than, amount, count on, count back, put together, add together, total, take away, How many altogether? How many are left?

Provide opportunities for children to see a number name linked to a set of objects in which the objects are grouped into tens and ones, so that they begin to understand place value in numbers to 50. Ordinal language can be modelled through real life opportunities, such as who is fourth, fifth…in a queue. Counting can be practised both forward and backwards from different points on the number sequence 0 – 50. Explore which of two numbers is bigger or smaller, both across a number track or line and when comparing sets of objects. Help children make sensible estimates.

Make sure children are secure in demonstrating numbers 1 to 10 on their fingers, as well as adding and subtracting on their fingers. Children should be able to hold one number in their head and then count on or backwards using their fingers. Subtraction can be modelled by placing numbers along a number track and then removing them as you count back.

Stage 6: 0 – 100

Stage 6 extends the number range up to 100. Children will become more secure counting forwards and backwards in twos, fives and tens. Key vocabulary includes: number, count, pattern, forwards, backwards, next, before, between, sequence, number, names to 100, multiple, What number comes next?, What is the number before…? Count in twos, fives, tens., count on, count back, order, add together, add, total, take away, subtract, difference, How many altogether?, How many are left?, What is the difference between?

Children should be encouraged to count forward and backwards in the number sequence – in ones, twos, fives and tens. Models such as number lines, number tracks and hundreds grids can be used to visually display the sequence and to identify numbers before, after and between given numbers. Use small numbers when initially adding and taking away so that the major focus is on the calculation strategy, rather than counting large numbers.

Other Number Concepts

Each stage of mathematics provides a progression from simple counting and number patterns to more advanced calculation. Each stage covers a group of numbers children are familiar with, and these number ranges are expanded as the stages of mathematics progress. After completing these 6 stages, number knowledge can be expanded from 0 – 1000. Furthermore, other number concepts that require direct instruction can be introduced. These are place value, calculation, and fractions, percentages and decimals. Appendix 2 shows the Stages of Mathematics.

Place Value

Place value is the value of where the digit is in the number, such as units, tens, hundreds, and thousands. So for 3,452 the place value of the 5 is tens. Children can be taught to recognise that the position of a digit gives its value and that zero is a place holder, as in 100 which represents one hundred, zero tens and zero units. An understanding of place value will enable children to count on and back in tens or hundreds from any two or three digit number.

Key vocabulary for place value includes: units, tens, hundreds, thousands, millions, zero, rounding up, rounding down, multiply by 10 or 100, divide by 10 or 100. Children can read, write and order whole numbers by recognising that the position of a digit gives its value. The symbols $<$, $>$, $=$ can be introduced to show relationships between numbers. Moving across the place value can be demonstrated through multiplying and dividing numbers by 10 or 100. Children can also practise rounding numbers to the nearest 10 or 100 and then 1000.

Calculation

Children can make decisions about which operations and problem-solving strategies to use. They will develop rapid recall of number facts including addition and subtraction facts to 10 and use these to derive facts with totals to 20. They will also learn multiplication facts for the x2 and x10 multiplication tables and derive corresponding division facts, know doubles of numbers to 10 and halves of even numbers to 20. From here they can develop a range of mental methods for finding, from known facts, those that they cannot recall, including adding 10 to any single-digit number, then adding and subtracting a multiple of 10 to or from a two-digit number. This provides a variety of methods for adding and subtracting.

Children can also understand that addition can be done in any order and that subtraction is the inverse of addition. Multiplication is repeated addition and halving is the inverse of doubling. They will begin to understand division as grouping repeated subtraction.

Key vocabulary includes: problem, solution, puzzle, pattern, methods, sign, operation, symbol, number sentence, equation, mental calculation, written calculation, informal method, jottings, diagrams, pictures, images, add, plus, sum, total, subtract, take away, minus, difference, double, halve, inverse, multiply, times, multiplied by, product, multiple, share, share equally, divide, divided by, divided into, left, left over, remainder.

Children can apply their understanding that the difference between two numbers will stay the same if both numbers are reduced or increased by the same amount. For example, the difference between 123 and 117 is the same as the difference between 23 and 17, the answer in each case is 6. Likewise, the sum of two numbers stays the same when one of the numbers is increased by an amount and the other is decreased by the same amount. For example, $25 + 55$ is the same as $15 + 65$. Finally, numbers can be separated by their place values. $285 - 54$ can be represented as $285 - 50 - 4$, and $345 + 54$ as $345 + 50 + 4$. Children can bridge through 100 where necessary, for example for $141 - 79$ give 21 to 79 to make 100 and a further 41 to 100 to make 141, a difference of $41 + 21 = 62$.

When children first develop an understanding of multiplication and division they can describe the effects on the place value of digits when multiplying one and two digit numbers by 10 and 100. They will need to learn multiplication facts for the two, three, four, five, six and ten times tables. From here, they can partition two-digit numbers into its tens and ones and use a grid to help them record the calculation steps. For example $14 \times 4 = (10 \times 4) + (4 \times 4) = 56$.

Practical examples can be used to explain operations. For example, 20 pens are shared equally into 4 cups. How many pens will be in each cup? $20 \div 4 = 5$. As they become proficient, children should be able to generate inverse statements to work out missing numbers. For example $32 \div 4 = 8$ can be re-written as $32 = 4 \times 8$.

Fractions, Decimals and Percentages

Children need an understanding of unit fractions (for example, one-third, or one-half) then fractions that are several parts of a whole (for example, three-quarters). From here, they can recognise the equivalence between the decimal and fraction forms of one half, quarters, tenths and hundredths.

Decimals become an extension of place value to explain tenths, hundreds, and thousandths. Percentages mean the number of parts per 100 and can be used for comparisons. Key vocabulary includes: fraction, part, equal parts, one whole, one half, one third, one quarter, one fifth, one sixth, one tenth, decimal, unit, tenth, hundredth, thousand, percentage, 10 percent, 20 percent, 100 percent.

Fractions, decimals and percentages can be presented in contexts such as parts of a whole in pizzas, money, measurements, and number of people. They can also be displayed on a number line. Children should be encouraged to round a number to one or two decimal places or to add and subtract fractions. At a higher level, fraction equivalence can be taught and children can reduce fractions to their lowest form (for example, $4/8 = \frac{1}{2}$).

Figure 6.6 Fraction Manipulatives
Fraction Fortress is a fraction tower building game. Fraction maipulatives allow children to visualise relationships across fraction pieces. Children can also practise adding and subtracting fraction segments.

Summary

Numbers are all around us. The mathematical brain develops two circuits for processing numbers: a dorsal 'quantitative' circuit involved with manipulation of number facts and a ventral 'memorised calculation' circuit in charge of long-term store for number facts. Often, a combination of the two circuits is engaged as children access calculations they know from rote and manipulate these to comprise the answers they need.

Children can learn number patterns systematically moving from small numbers through to three and four digit numbers. Visual mathematics, manipulatives and multi-sensory learning supports this process. At a higher level they will learn about place value, calculations (multiplication and division) and fractions, percentages and decimals. They can also learn to manipulate these concepts and to move between language and quantitative forms of number representations.

7

Brains that Work Differently

Each brain's connections are as individual as a set of fingerprints. Some brains learn very quickly, and soon move ahead of their age. Other brains find learning difficult, no matter how hard they try. Reluctant learners are sometimes overlooked and considered unmotivated or lazy. Indeed, emotional issues can arise as they see themselves fall further behind their peers. In some case, they may put in extra effort just to keep up with their peers, but this extra effort is often unnoticed.

Different Genes

Learning difficulties run in families and are shown to have a strong genetic component. Human genome research provides extensive databases of genes and anomalies in chunks of DNA. A mutation in gene KIAA0319 (on Chromosome 6) has been reported in two of the most common learning difficulties, specific language impairment and dyslexia. Two further candidate genes for dyslexia are DYX1C1 (on Chromosome 15) and DCDC2 (both on Chromosome 6). These genes appear to play an important role in the migration of neurons when the brain is forming during the third trimester. They express in the 6th month of pregnancy when the foetal brain undergoes a pruning process where brain cells migrate to form connections with other brain cells.

The other gene marked to learning difficulties is ROBO1 (on Chromosome 3). Although its role is not completely understood, it is believed to be involved with malformations of the corpus callosum, the fibre track that links the left and right hemispheres.[30]

Post mortem studies of adults with dyslexia have revealed some intriguing findings. Ectopias, neurons that are not placed correctly, are observed in the brains of those with learning difficulties. These ectopias are reported to be peppered all over the learning regions and areas of the left brain in those with dyslexia. The effect during foetal brain development is a disruption to neural migration, leaving messy piles of neurons and other neurons that have travelled past their expected position and crashed.[31]

Structural imaging studies of living brains with dyslexia confirm these differences. They show a profound disorganisation of the left brain with grey matter being rare in some places and extremely dense in others.[32] Interestingly, the size and quantity of abnormalities seems to nicely predict the level of learning difficulty.

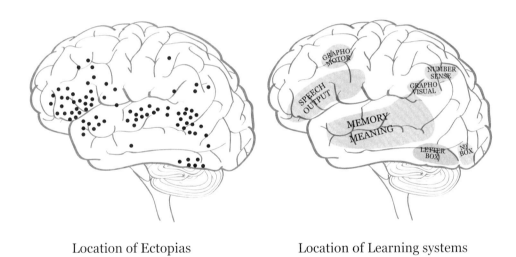

Location of Ectopias   Location of Learning systems

Figure 7.1 Ecotopias and Learning Systems
Ecotopias have been observed in the brains of those with learning difficulties during post mortem autopsy investigations (Galaburda et al., 1985). Interestingly, the location of ectopias overlaps the location of learning systems and explains the observed behavioural difficulties observed during development.

Dys-Constellation

The concept of a dys-constellation is used to explain a family of learning difficulties.[33] Within a typical school there are groups of children with mixed abilities, not only in terms of life experiences, but in terms of their neurological wiring. Some children have problems with reading (dyslexia), some with co-ordination (dyspraxia) and some with handwriting (dysgraphia). Others have problems with oral language (specific language impairment), with spelling (dysorthographia) or with mathematics (dyscalculia). All of these learning difficulties are observed across families.

It is believed that the location of the cortical disruption (i.e. ectopias) in children with learning difficulties will influence the type (or types) of learning difficulty they have. The precise location of each ectopia is under genetic control. Specific learning difficulties (in the dys-constellation) have a complex genetic aetiology involving several regions of different chromosomes.

Some genes control a child's susceptibility to ectopias (common learning difficulty genes) and other genes control the specific brain locations where ectopias will form (specific to the individual learning difficulty). For example, KIAA0319 is present in both dyslexia and SLI (common learning difficulty gene, presumably a creator of ectopias), whereas DYX1C1 and DCDC2 are specific to dyslexia (perhaps to the location of where ectopias will form). Together these genes will express what learning difficulty a child has and how severe it is.

The causality of genes, to ectopias, to cortical disruption, to behaviour is also seen in mice. About half of New Zealand black mice show ectopias which they inherit genetically. There are learning differences between those mice that have ectopias and those that don't. A mouse's difficulty in maze learning tasks is dependent on where the location of ectopias had formed.[34] This animal model predicts what happens in children with learning difficulties.

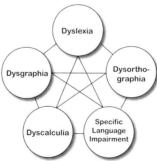

Figure 7.2 Dys-constellation
The dys-constellation describes a common neighbourhood of learning difficulties, high prevalence of co-morbidities, and common origins.

Dyslexia

Dyslexia is a reading impairment that manifests itself as a difficulty in phonological processing. Children with dyslexia have problems with grapheme-to-phoneme conversion (or sounding out words).[35] Their neural disruption is to the dorsal reading circuit which maps letters onto sounds.

In all countries, the same number of children carry a genetic predisposition to dyslexia. However, the manifestation of dyslexia is determined by the orthography that underlies language. As English is an opaque language, there will be more dyslexics observed in English schools than Italian schools where the language is transparent. Nevertheless, it is possible to identify dyslexia in Italy by testing large populations and recording reading and decoding speeds.

One such study did manage to find a sample of Italian dyslexics and compared them to English and French dyslexics with a reading task during brain-imaging. The results revealed a biological unity of dyslexia, with all adult dyslexics showing significant under-activation of left-brain reading circuits in comparison to matched controls. The same degree of under-activation was noted for all three nationalities.[36]

Interestingly, structural brain scans also showed an abnormal increase in grey matter density around these reading areas which correlated to the reading impairment.[37] Studies with dyslexic children point to under-activation of the same regions, with brain dysfunction correlating to the severity of the reading deficit. There are now hundreds of brain-imaging studies of dyslexia, including PET, fMRI, MEG, EEG and Diffusor Imaging.[38] All converge on the same regions that show under-activation in the reading circuits of the left brain, giving the brain based model of dyslexia considerable support.

Not all dyslexics have phonological processing difficulties. A small sub-type of dyslexia called surface dyslexia has problems with visual memory of whole word configurations, without necessarily showing the hallmark phonological deficit. These children have problems reading irregular words and often make regularisation errors (where they sound out the irregular word as if it was regular).[39] Surface dyslexics are expected to have neural disruption to the ventral reading circuit, in particular the brain's letterbox. Brain studies comparing surface and phonological dyslexics do show differences in activation supporting the different behavioural patterns observed. Twin studies also suggest a different genetic pattern between the two groups. Future genetic studies may confirm common dyslexia genes (leading to ectopias) and discover specific sub-type genes (determining disruption to either dorsal or ventral reading circuits or both).

Dysgraphia

Dysgraphia is a transcription deficiency that primarily affects handwriting. Specifically, it is a difficulty in orthographic coding and the processing of letters in words for motor production of handwriting. It is independent of reading abilities and intelligence.[40]

Use of the orthographic loop involves taking words from the mind's eye and producing sequential finger movements to write the letters, with feedback from the eye. The neural disruption in dysgraphia is to the writing circuit which links the parietal lobe (visual letter shape) to Exner's area in the front of the brain (letter motor movements).

Although there aren't any brain-imaging studies of development dysgraphia currently available, one study to investigate Chinese dyslexia provides interesting results that may be relevant to dysgraphia. This study compared Chinese dyslexics with the results of the British, French and Italian dyslexics in the previously described study. Their converging results also showed a drop in activation of the reading circuits in the left brain, however more marked was a reduced activation in Exner's writing area.[41]

Chinese dyslexics, who must commit three thousand characters to motor memory, may have difficulty accessing these writing gestures in working memory, which in turn reduces their reading skill. It is possible that alphabetic writing systems create dyslexics with phonological problems and Asian writing systems create dyslexics with graphomotor problems. Perhaps Asian dysgraphics are more likely to become dyslexics based on the Chinese orthography. Future brain-imaging research will hopefully explore this further.

Dysorthographia

Dysorthographia is a developmental spelling difficulty. It is the spelling equivalent of dyslexia and is sometimes used interchangeably with dyslexia. The affected circuits are the dorsal and ventral reading circuits, but in the reverse direction.

Two subtypes of dysorthograpia can be described, and these overlay onto the definitions of phonological and surface dyslexia. Dysphonetics have difficulty encoding (using the dorsal spelling circuit). Their spelling patterns are not phonologically consistent (no use of invented spellings) and they must rely on sight vocabulary for spelling words.

Dyseidetics tend to spell phonetically but inaccurately. Their difficulties are with spelling irregular words (which must be memorised) and come from problems recalling words or forming them in the brain's letterbox. Brain studies of dysphonetics and dyseidetics show different activation patterns suggesting different compensation strategies.[42] Again, future genetic research may discover common dysorthographic genes with secondary genes predicting the subtype of spelling impairment (depending on the location of ectopic disruptions).

Dyscalculia

Dyscalculia is a specific learning difficulty that affects the ability to process numbers and the acquisition of mathematics. Although children with dyscalculia have had the same opportunities to learn as other children, they encounter difficulties in mastering the basics of mathematical thinking. More specifically, there are difficulties with manipulation of numbers on the brain's internal number line. These difficulties include the understanding and manipulation of numbers, counting sequences backwards, a relative difficulty for subtraction over addition, or a need to write down equations without performing them in one's head.[43] Further difficulties may also include problems with time, measurement, spatial reasoning and left/right confusion.

Dyscalculia does not necessarily affect the ability to excel at high level mathematics and in fact, some of these children may go on to be gifted in abstract mathematical reasoning. Early signs of dyscalculia are difficulties in subitising (working out the numbers of up to four objects from a brief glance without counting them). The neural disruption associated with dyscalculia is the number sense area in the parietal lobe.

Brain-imaging research investigating dyscalculia shows under-activation of this area. There are equal numbers of boys and girls with dyscalculia. 50% of the siblings of students with dyscalculia are also expected to have it. Although research suggests a genetic basis to dyscalculia, research into the neural basis of dyscalculia and the underlying genes is in its infancy.

It is possible that not all children with dyscalculia have difficulty with manipulating numbers. Some with impairment to the ventral 'memorised calculation' circuit may have a memory or retrieval deficit. Such students may have relative strength in the dorsal 'quantitative' circuit enabling them to perform manipulations on their internal number lines, but will have difficulty memorising these equations and committing them to rote verbal memory. Even more so, the ability to memorize times-tables will be severely impaired. Such students will take considerably more time to complete mathematical problem solving and will be over-reliant on the dorsal 'quantitative' circuit for working out the answer.

Specific Language Impairment

Specific Language Impairment involves abnormal language development which cannot be accounted for by slow development, brain damage or sensory problems.[44] SLI children start speaking later than usual and are often delayed in forming sentences. They have difficulty using verbs and tenses. A variety of oral language components can be affected including grammar, semantics and phonological development and subtypes have been described around expressive and receptive language themes.

It is accepted that SLI is a genetic condition, with strong evidence coming from twin studies. Here, while identical twins sharing the same genes tend to show very similar language abilities, non identical twins may differ considerably in their language ability despite sharing the same environment. 50 to 70% of children with SLI have at least one other family member with the learning difficulty.[45]

A family study of SLI with brain imaging showed under-activation of temporal and frontal lobes in SLI during language tasks when compared to non-SLI.[46] According to the brain-based model it is these regions where we would expect to find ectopias or neural disruptions.

Co-Morbidity

Co-morbidity is the medical term for two difficulties that occur at the same time. Logically, children who have difficulty with reading will most likely have problems with spelling. Children with specific language impairment will have problems expressing complex thoughts in writing. Reading difficulties may also affect mathematical performance when tasks involve a strong language component, and those with handwriting difficulties often show co-morbid spelling difficulties. Thus, co-morbidities are expected, although not always present, due to the inter-relation of learning circuits in the left brain.

Multiple learning difficulties may be common as ectopias have disrupted a wide range of shared circuits and regions in the left brain. Depending on where the ectopias have formed will determine if reading, spelling, listening, speaking, writing or mathematics abilities are spared. Thus, it is possible to have a student who has specific learning difficulties with spelling and reading, but who is gifted at mathematics. Another student may have poor handwriting but have very good language skills. Every child with specific learning difficulties has a unique pattern of strengths and weaknesses depending on where their ectopias are located.

Dyspraxia

Dyspraxia is a learning difficulty that affects the planning of movement and co-ordination. It is neurological in origin and again cannot be explained by developmental delay or other sensory problems. More general problems may include remembering instructions and deadlines, losing things, problems completing tasks and organizing one's time, at least beyond what would be expected as normal.

Animal studies may help to explain the neurological roots to dyspraxia. Freeze lesions to the foetal rat brain during development also lead to disrupted neural migration (used to mimic the effect of ectopias). Again, the location of cortical disruption influences the spatial learning difficulties the rat will acquire. However, independent of the exact location of neural disruption in the rat brain are further disruptions to sub-brain structures such as the thalamus which leads to sensory impairment. Evidence of sensory impairment comes from further tests of auditory discrimination in post freeze-lesion rats. Hormonal conditions seem to moderate this effect. Increased testosterone in male rats leads to increased disruption to the thalamus creating further sensory impairments.[47]

If the animal model predicts what happens in humans, this could explain why we see gross motor symptoms in children with learning difficulties. Ectopias in the left brain lead to specific learning difficulties, depending on their location. However, further disruption occurs beyond the left brain to the thalamus and magnocellular cells that feed from the thalamus to the cerebellum (a separate structure attached to the bottom of the brain involved in motor control). This further disruption is intensified under hormone conditions suggesting: 1) males are more likely to exhibit additional motor deficits and 2) co-morbidity with motor deficits and other learning difficulties.

What we see in the classroom seems to fit nicely with this view. Dyspraxia is more common in males, affecting 4 males to every 1 female. Dyspraxia also shows high co-morbidity with other learning difficulties.[48] Co-morbidities are often observed with dyslexia, dysorthographia, dyscalculia, dysgraphia and specific language impairment. As would be predicted by the location of ectopias, dyspraxia varies widely from child to child where some will have reading, spelling or mathematics problems, while others will have strong reading, spelling or mathematic skills.

Even the subtypes of dyspraxia suggest co-morbid patterns. Verbal dyspraxia involves linguistic or phonological impairment (overlapping with SLI and dyslexia). Fine motor dyspraxia suggests problems with handwriting (overlapping with dysgraphia). Coordination dyspraxia describes a more pure form involving poor gross motor skills, timing, balance and difficulties remembering, combining and sequencing movements. Such coordination problems are often observed in children with learning difficulties.[49]

Interestingly, some theories of dyslexia point to the magnocellular system and the cerebellum[50] as causes of dyslexia, to explain the dyspraxic patterns observed in these children. According to how ectopias can affect secondary structures, such patterns would be expected in dyslexia, especially dyslexic boys. However, they are not causal of the dyslexia as the real cause is the ectopias that have disrupted the reading circuits of the left brain. Rather, mild motor impairments are a secondary consequence resulting from how the ectopia (with the influence of hormones) has gone on to impact on the thalamus, magnocellur cells and cerebellum.[51]

When intervention programmes target balancing and coordination activities to overcome a reading problem they are really targeting the secondary problem. Coordination activities may help raise self-confidence in children with learning difficulties, but they should not replace good reading interventions that target the left-brain reading circuits.

Scotopic Sensitivity Syndrome

Scotopic Sensitivity Syndrome (also referred to as Visual Stress and Irlen's Syndrome) is a visual perceptual disorder that affects reading and writing abilities. Children with scotopic sensitivity syndrome (SSS) are reported to experience difficulty reading because they see busy patterns, stripes and rivers of white on the page. The text also may appear to move and words can come together making them unrecognisable. It is believed that some signals from the eye are not getting to the brain in their proper form and on time, resulting in a visual perceptual disorder. This may be accounted for by hypersensitive visual pathways that are reacting incorrectly to certain wavelengths of light. If the brain receives a double exposed image, the location of items can be confused and minor errors can occur such as letters moving around on the page.

The ectopia model can be extended to explain co-morbidity of learning difficulties with SSS. Secondary hormonal disruption to the thalamus and magnocellur cells that extend to the parietal cortex may disrupt the brains 'where' visual pathway.[52] Such a disruption could explain why children with specific learning difficulties continue to make b and d letter reversals, even as they get older. Although as a secondary consequence of dyslexia, some refer to SSS as a form of dyslexia.

The use of colour overlays improves the visual perception and subsequent reading abilities in some children with SSS. Thus, vision therapy and coloured lens can be beneficial to children with SSS, but should not be used to replace reading based interventions for those who have co-morbid dyslexia. This sensory perception problem observed in SSS is also common in many (but not all) children with autism.

ADHD

Attention Deficit Hyperactivity Disorder (ADHD) is a behavioural disorder of inattention, hyperactivity and impulsiveness or a combination of these. Subtypes include inattentive, hyperactive/impulsive, or a mixed subtype of the two. ADHD results in restlessness, impulsive actions, and an inability to focus which impedes the ability to learn. Children with ADHD have difficulties sitting still in class and concentrating on school work. It is two to four times more frequent in boys than girls.[53]

Twin studies show that ADHD is genetic in origin and can explain 75% of cases. Complication during pregnancy and birth may play a non-genetic role. Genetic research suggests ADHD cases arise from mutant genes that affect dopamine receptors. Dopamine pathways in the brain provide biochemical reward mechanisms.[54] Disruptions to these reward pathways mean children with ADHD are more likely to succeed at tasks that are inherently motivating. Other boring tasks are hard to focus on for children with ADHD because of low dopamine levels.

The neurobiology of ADHD shows different abnormalities to specific learning difficulties. Although it is possible that ectopias may explain some cases of ADHD, a scientific link has not been established. Within the structures of the brain, ADHD features include reduced volume of the prefrontal cortex. This suggests that inattention, hyperactivity and impulsivity may reflect differences in how the frontal lobe works for children with ADHD.

Two thirds of children with ADHD have a co-morbid specific learning difficulty.[55] It is difficult to know if their learning difficulties stem from specific learning difficulty genes and thus ectopias, or alternatively that behavioural problems disrupt the learning of cognitive skills such as reading and mathematics. Future brain research into specific learning difficulties should separate co-morbid ADHD from pure groups to examine differences in activation patterns, especially in response to interventions.

Learning Delayed

Learning delayed children fail to reach their developmental milestones by the expected period of time. Slow development in one area (such as language) is often related to low growth in other areas (such as social / emotional development). The warning signs of learning delay include: behavioural problems, gross motor difficulties, visual perceptual problems, and language delay.

Academically, learning delayed children struggle with speaking, reading, spelling, writing and mathematics. The plasticity of the brain allows many children who are delayed to catch up. Learning delay is not specific to one area of the brain and seems to impact on the aggregate including cognitive, emotional and perceptual-motor systems.

Potential causes of learning delay are both genetic and environmental. Genetic causes include chromosomal abnormality, such as Down syndrome, or mutant genes, such as autism. Environmental factors can influence brain development before birth, such as poor maternal nutrition, infections or exposure to toxins. After birth environmental factors include premature birth, severe poverty, poor nutrition or a lack of care.

Autism

Autism is characterised by difficulties in communication, social interaction, as well as restrictive and repetitive patterns of behaviour.[56] Children with autism can demonstrate a lack of empathy and social reciprocity, and show impaired non-verbal behaviours such as lack of eye contact or facial expression.[57] This can make it difficult to have shared enjoyments and to develop friendships. In some cases they may show superior skills in visual perception and attention, relative to the general population.

Highly functioning autism children show normal, or above normal spelling and vocabulary skills. However, figurative language, inference and comprehension scores are considerably lower. Children with autism may be poorly co-ordinated, have poor handwriting, poor balance, or problems with visual-motor integration.

Common symptoms are often seen across families, suggesting a strong genetic origin, although no specific genes have yet been directly identified. Different mechanisms behind brain re-organisation are believed to be at work in autism in comparison to ADHD and specific learning difficulties. The neurology of autism appears to affect the neuronal connectivity across all functional brain systems, rather than localised, specific ones. Differences are believed to develop during foetal development where abnormal neural migration changes the connectivity and final structure of the brain.

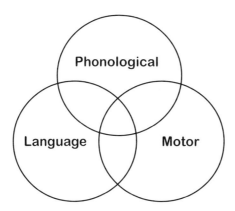

Figure 7.3 Common Core Deficits
Phonological, motor and language difficulties are often observed in children with learning difficulties.

Overcoming Learning Difficulties

Brain imaging can be used to demonstrate the benefits of effective intervention. There are two results from successful intervention, normalization and compensation. Effective training in all studies shows an increase in activation in the brain. Brain plasticity can contribute to successful intervention.

For reading intervention, increased activation is observed in the dorsal reading circuit and the letterbox, suggesting a normalization of brain function.[58] Other areas shown to activate specific to dyslexia are the frontal lobe (Broca's area) and right opposite areas of the left temporal and parietal lobes.[59] These findings are interpreted as compensatory strategies. Presumably the frontal lobe is activated in explicit speech production strategies and working memory. Areas in the right brain that light up are a compensatory reliance on analogous regions that are not affected by neural disruption. The right brain may contain unaffected networks that are capable of performing or supporting the subprocesses involved in reading.

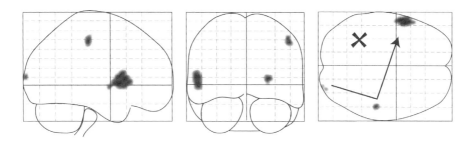

Figure 7.4 Dyslexic Compensation
During phonologial processing this dyslexic subject showed increased activation on the back of the right hemipshere and in the front of the left hemisphere. Dyslexic compensation appears to bypass faulty circuits in the back of the left brain by utilising unaffected right hemisphere circuits along with an increase of activation in the front of the brain (Milne et al, 2002).

Compensation may be further explained by the animal model. By disrupting cell migration in rodents with the microscopic lesions, abnormal connections with other regions of the brain begin to form. If the left brain is disrupted, extra connections can be formed across to the right brain. When we extend this to the model of dyslexia, ectopic disruptions to the left brain are expected to result in extra connections to the right brain across analogous regions. In agreement with this an enlargement of the corpus callosum is observed in dyslexia and right brain activations are seen in functionality.

Distal Causes of Learning Difficulties

As children with different brains receive the same learning interventions as each other, do we need labels such as specific learning difficulty, ADHD, autism or learning delayed? They are useful, as parents (and children) like to know the origins of learning problems. Some brains are different for neurological reasons. Children can be born with differences – genetically inherited conditions that lead to differences in structure and function. As they learn to overcome their difficulties they engage in strategies that are unlikely to ever be as efficient as their peers. Thus, these people have the right to know what is going on, although labelling children should be done carefully. If brain-based information is not included we can never be completely certain of the assessment.

Figure 7.5 Children's Book on Dyslexia
How My Brain Learns to Read is a children's book (and available as an iPad app) on reading and the brain. It also covers dyslexia in a child-friendly way, with visual brain examples and analogies, so that children can understand why they may be having difficulties learning to read.

What should be done if a child shows the symptoms of learning difficulties? With the help of an educational psychologist, a full assessment of his or her learning strengths and weaknesses should be undertaken. Assessment records of children across their development provide powerful clues to the learning profile and can help rule out the possibility of developmental delay. When the student reaches higher education, a history of learning difficulties may provide evidence for special examination conditions.

Many learning disabled adults shy away from these conditions, as they want to be treated like everyone else. Nevertheless, it is sometimes appropriate to make special examination conditions available considering the extra energy consumed by their brains as they perform cognitive tasks such as reading, spelling, writing and calculating. It would seem ridiculous for a dyscalculia student not to have access to calculator, a dysorthographic student not to be able to use a spell checker, and a dysgraphic student not to be able to use a word processor. Higher learning is not about retesting these elementary processes!

Creativity

In the hunter-gatherer days, neurological disruption would not have been a disadvantage for those with learning difficulties, as classroom learning was a long way away. Back then, brains with unusual wiring provided the tribe with another way of thinking about things (like using a boomerang when everyone else had a spear). Tasks like developing weapons for hunting or new tools for farming may have required the brain to think differently. This is why ectopic disruption to neural networks can be considered an important part of evolution. Ectopias don't damage the brain, but wire it in a completely different way. Having different types of problem solvers within the group is essential. By having both normal and 'neurologically disrupted' brains working in the same team, synergies lead to better problem solving. New ideas can be discussed, debated and created from different angles and with different points of view.[60]

Those with ADHD also make an important contribution to the group. Groups need members who are more proficient at taking risks, competing and behaving unpredictably. We can imagine an ADHD and a dyslexic leaving the tribe together to explore an undiscovered area, and in doing so find a new food source which they can then bring back and share with the group. In today's world, those with learning differences can excel in creative fields by changing the existing paradigm.

For those with highly functioning autism, their 'eye for detail' can be an advantage in the fields of mathematics, computing, engineering and science. Society needs different brains – everyone benefits. Anecdotal evidence points to a long list of scientists with creative strengths who were reluctant learners. They contributed to society by thinking differently and developing new ways of doing things. Famous people who struggled with learning include Leonardo da Vinci, Albert Einstein and Winston Churchill to name just a few. Even cognitive neuroscience is grateful. After overcoming their learning difficulties, Michael Faraday, James Maxwell and Nikola Tesla each contributed to discovering the principles behind today's modern brain imaging!

Summary

Evolution wants diversity and gives society a number of brains that work differently. Often, they may have the similar language, phonology or gross motor problems, but for different reasons. A family of brains that work differently come from genes that create ectopias which disrupt how neurons are wired in the foetus. Referred to as the dys-constellation, this family includes dyslexia, specific language impairment, dysorthographia, dysgraphia and dyscalculia. A closely related cousin is dyspraxia, which is commonly co-morbid with these specific learning difficulties and is likely to stem from the same genes as a secondary consequence of ectopic disruption. The same is true for scotopic sensitivity syndrome.

Another brain that works differently is the ADHD brain. It also has genetic roots, but these genes disrupt the formation of the pre-frontal cortex and the brains reward systems. The ADHD brain is resistant to traditional educational methods and requires increased stimulation if it is to acquire the skills of reading, spelling, writing and mathematics. Although ADHD children often show learning difficulties, they can overcome these if the learning conditions are right.

Autistic children also have genetic origins to their different brains and have learning difficulties as a result. Finally, learning delayed children can have genetic or environmental causes that prevent them from reaching their milestones, again resulting in learning difficulties. Despite the various distal causes, interventions are the same for all brains that work differently, high in educational content and multi-sensory learning. Finally, brains that work differently are here for a reason. They give us different operating systems that solve problems in different ways. Everyone can benefit from their creativity.

8

Teaching the Brain

The essential cognitive operations of speaking, reading, spelling, writing and mathematics each relate to an array of different learning circuits in the brain. When children are born their brains are highly plastic and open to change through education. Explicit teaching is required for children to consciously understand a concept and make connections across the left brain. However, not all children learn at the same rate and some children will have brains that work differently. By understanding the specific needs of individual children, teaching programmes can be customised to support successful approaches for all.

Scaffolding

Scaffolding is a teaching strategy that provides support to facilitate learning. It involves temporary help for children as they work towards reaching their next level. When competency increases, scaffolding is reduced and eventually withdrawn. At this point children have become independent or self-regulated. In the classroom, scaffolds include direct instruction, modelling, hints, partial solutions, cues and thinking aloud.[61] Scaffolding is designed to motivate the learner, simplify the task and provide direction. It reduces confusion with a clear step-by-step approach to learning. Children will begin to internalise learning as they use inner speech to construct an understanding of the learning concept. Inner speech can be used for 'think-aloud' modelling when approaching a future problem.

Zone of Proximal Development

The Zone of Proximal Development (ZOPD) is the learning distance between what the child can do with scaffolding, over and above what the child can do working independently. By providing learning assistance from scaffolding, a child can complete more complex tasks. Thus, the ZOPD is the extra learning that can be achieved for the child with the help of scaffolding. When children are working within their ZOPDs, their learning potentials are expanded.

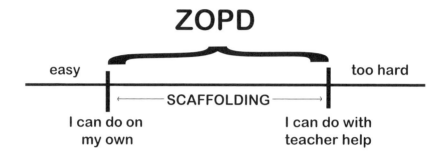

Figure 8.1 Zone of Proximal Development
The Zone of Proximal Development (ZOPD) is the distance between what children can do independently and what they can acheive with teacher help. The ZOPD represents scaffolding which can come from direct teaching support and instruction, or from techniques designed to accelerate learning..

Examples of Scaffolding

Children initially learn by imitating adults. When children are first learning to speak, parents are consistently modelling or scaffolding the correct use of vocabulary and grammar. This enables children to increase their ZOPDs as they master new words and structures. As parents read stories to their children they are engaging in the processes of language and comprehension, again expanding their ZOPDs. During reading instruction, they can use decodeable texts as a form of scaffolding (where the words are chosen for their phonological consistency based on the letters a child has systematically been taught).

The synthetic phonics progression provides scaffolding as it gradually introduces new letters and involves word building with letters previously taught. Guided reading is used to extend children's reading skills as the text is set at 90% - 95% accuracy. This distance from the independent reading level (95%) is the ZODP, which is extended through teaching support. Scaffolding is provided as children read unknown words, guiding them to the sounding-out strategy and helping them with blending the sounds together.

Scaffolding is also offered during guided writing, for example when a child is prompted to change a meaning or structure. Rather than coming up with a new sentence for the child, scaffolding involves helping the child create that sentence for themselves. Guided writing support helps children reach further than their independent writing, expanding their ZODPs. In spelling, children can be asked 'how to change run to running?' If they are not sure, they can be asked 'what's the rule?' to remind them that there is a rule, or provide part of the rule such as 'what do we need to do to stop the 'i' in 'ing' from making the 'u' in 'run' from saying it's name'.

Finally in mathematics, scaffolding can be used to guide learning, for example 'look at that number in the ten's position, does that look right?' Casual conversations between the child and the teacher provide an abundance of opportunities for scaffolding. Such interactions also provide opportunities for positive feedback to motivate the learner.

Accelerated Learning

The goal of accelerated learning is to help children learn faster and remember more. New approaches for accelerating learning include multi-sensory, informal, camouflage, blended and personalised learning. Each of these approaches can be thought of in terms of scaffolding and pushing out the ZOPD. Here, accelerated learning techniques enable the teacher to extend the ZOPD beyond its present limitations into new territory that was previously beyond the learning reach of the child.

Accelerated learning is achieved by increasing scaffolding, a conceptualisation different from popular 'accelerated learning' that often refers to different learning style preferences. Some regard this approach as a 'wasted effort' as rather than separating teaching into three different styles (visual, auditory and kinaesthetic) it makes more sense to integrate all efforts into a multi-sensory approach.

Other new approaches work on the principles of accelerated learning and encourage learning by doing. Unfortunately, unlike what is often suggested, there is very little brain research backing the effectiveness of accelerated learning. Rather, teachers are utilising these approaches because they work. In some cases, they may make all the difference between success and failure. As cognitive neuroscience is in its relative infancy, education has the ability to influence neuroscience here. Such an approach will contribute to the best designed experiments that can explore the beneficial effects of accelerated learning. This research will also be able to control the spread of neuro-myths, (such as teaching to a student in only one sensory style) and give some much needed validity to effective approaches such as multi-sensory learning.

Multi-Sensory Learning

Multi-sensory learning is a teaching method that makes learning easier for the child by utilising different senses including visual, auditory and kinaesthetic. Teacher resources high in multi-sensory learning are believed to stimulate, synchronise and harmonise multiple brain processes. Multi-sensory activities feature strongly in high quality teaching and often encompass, variously, simultaneous visual, auditory and kinaesthetic activities involving, for example, physical movement to support learning concepts. The multisensory approach can be integrated into lesson plans and activities as a form of scaffolding. For example, colour-coded letters, makes it is easier for children to see how consonants are different to vowels and how these patterns can be grouped together to make words.

One pioneering brain-imaging study has investigated the beneficial effects of multi-sensory learning.[62] Poor readers often have problems with auditory discrimination. This experiment showed when sound discrimination was taught with related visual patterns, the visual component enabled auditory learning, improving auditory discrimination and simultaneously improving reading skills. The behavioural result was accompanied by a normalization of the brain wave pattern for auditory discrimination.

Figure 8.2 Teaching Numeracy with Multi-Sensory Learning
Ten Frame Towers is a multi-sensosry game for teaching number patterns. Numbers are represented in ten frame shapes and these are overlaid or stacked to represent different mathematical patterns or relationships. Each ten frame is also colour coded as part of the multi-disciplinary approach.

Informal Learning

Informal learning occurs when children pick up a new concept or meaning from generalising outside of formal instruction. It is a natural, spontaneous form of learning that comes from observation, repetition, social interaction and problem solving. Sometimes, it can occur from making a mistake, or from being constrained by rules requiring adaptation. If the child wants to discover the solution to a problem, he or she may learn a number of facts 'naturally' along the journey.

Informal learning is enhanced when the journey is inherently fun. When children play numeracy or literacy games informally, they are practising turn taking, social interaction and learning from one another. This goes beyond what the activity is pedagogically trying to teach. It brings in reciprocal scaffolding where a group of children collaboratively work together and learn from each other's experiences. Another example is when a mother informally teachers her child language structures of syntax and morphology. Although she may not be explicitly aware of these rules, she can transfer them across to her child by modelling good speaking. The generation effect, often referred to as learning by doing, improves learning when something is actually created. For example, children are more likely to remember how to spell a new word after they have actually constructed it for themselves with moveable letters.

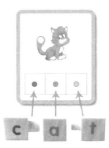

Figure 8.3 Teaching Consonant-Vowel-Consonant Patterns with Informal Learning
Children can learn informally by playing with Tri-blocks and word building cards. These cards are colour-coded to guide the direction of letter patterns (CVC) and answer is printed on the reverse so children can check to see if they are correct.

Camouflage Learning

Disguising a learning activity as a game is called camouflage learning. Effective instruction involves intense and prolonged training that also holds the child's motivation, attention and pleasure networks. Attention and reward systems can increase learning speed. Educational programmes must excite learning brains in the most appealing way. Stimulating activities will activate learning circuits more strongly. By amplifying learning circuits, children will be more engaged. This type of approach is beneficial to all children, but especially reluctant learners and those with ADHD.

Figure 8.4 Teaching Literacy and Numeracy with Camouflage Learning
Read Racers and Number Trucks incorparate teaching wheels into toy vehicles as part of camouflage learning. Children can remove each wheel and practise on it independently, or alternatively play with the wheels on the vehicles. As the wheel rotates it creates an equation or a spelling / reading activity. A slideable answer flap helps with self-correcting.

Blended Learning

Blended learning is the mixing of different learning environments, both face-to-face and computer based activities. This integrated approach brings in educational technologies such as computers, tablets, smart-phones, interactive whiteboards and emerging electronic media. Effective blended learning should be rich in pedagogy, knowledge and social interaction. It also provides flexibility, so that children can be self-paced based on their preferred speed and ability, as well as opportunities to catch-up at home if they have missed materials. Teachers can enhance their curriculum by blending learning with a number of digital resources.

Figure 8.5 Using iPad Techology for Blended Learning
Children grow up with technology and a naturally want to use it for learning. The Rainbow Phonics programme has been designed to follow a systematic synthetic phonics progression on the iPad. By using iPad technology children can follow this progression and unlock new letter sounds as they develop confidence and fluency. There is also a range of books and physical activities as part of the Rainbow Phonics programme. Multi-sensory approaches are blended across each medium.

Personalised Learning

Personalised learning rightly recognises differences in children's rate of learning and the need to provide work that is neither too easy nor too hard for each child (inside the Zone of Proximal Development). It requires programmes to be adapted to the specific needs of the child. Working inside the ZOPD provides levels that are difficult enough to engage the learner, yet easy enough to sustain enjoyment. Curriculum and pedagogy can be tailored to meet the needs or individual learners. The term technical scaffolding can be used to explain the role that technology may play in supporting success. Through personalised learning, the learner becomes a co-designer of the learning pathway.

Diversity and Inclusion

Diversity is the existence of many unique learners in the classroom. This includes children from different backgrounds, with different learning experiences, and different brains. Inclusion means a classroom environment where everyone has an opportunity to fully participate in the learning process, and where each child is valued for their individual skills, experiences and perspectives. Prevention and intervention methods include children with learning difficulties both within classroom teaching and as part of one-to-one work.[63]

Prevention

In a mainstream setting, prevention refers to whole class teaching that caters to the different and developing needs of all children, closing the gap between high and low achievers by preventing learning failure. The most important strategy for achieving prevention is to provide a teaching programme that is progressive, high quality and covers all the pedagogy needed to build the learning circuits of the left brain systematically. Quality first teaching will involve a blend of whole-class, group and individual work that provides optimal opportunities for scaffolding and accelerated learning. The benefits of reciprocal scaffolding are all too obvious as children engage in learning tasks that involve helping each other.

Intervention

Early failure can be overcome to a very large extent by timely intervention. The importance of responding early to such difficulties cannot be overstressed as research indicates that once entrenched, failure is much harder to reverse. It can also be detrimental to other areas of learning and self-esteem. Interventions must provide an early accurate assessment of children's knowledge and skills, with regular updating and tracking of progress. Assessment information should shape support. Data tracking children's progress can be used to assign teaching time and match resources.

The aim for children who have fallen behind is to reach the target levels for their age. Intervention programmes should be time limited and have clear entry and exit criteria. Effective intervention can come from a teaching assistant working in small groups, either within the class or outside. Parents can also be given guidance on how to help children at home. Support from parents is a notable feature of successful intervention programmes.

Children can be grouped according to their abilities and moved between groups depending on their progress. Intervention work should focus on skills children have already met in their mainstream classes but may involve more scaffolding to strengthen those aspects they didn't understand. All contributions must be implemented to an agreed plan that coordinates intervention and mainstream work. Intervention should have fidelity to the mainstream programme, but with some modifications, such as emphasising particular aspects of multi-sensory work to intensify support.

Levels of Causation

The terms proximal and distal causes come from the field of philosophy to describe close and distant causations. If a boat was sinking, the proximal cause could be that there was a hole in the hull. The distal cause explains where that hole came from. It may have come from lack of maintenance resulting in a crack, a failure to put the bung in, or from hitting a rock. However, it is the proximal cause that will be the most important thing. Finding where the hole is and blocking it - so that no more water can come in! The same is true for biological models. Various distal causes explain why some children have language, phonology, visual perception or co-ordination problems. The proximal cause is the actual circuits of the brain and how they are performing. If there is a problem, the intervention must fix it as soon as possible, without necessarily being overly concerned as to the distal causes of how the problem got there in the first place.

Distal Causes

All children have a combination of genetic and environmental factors that influence how their learning circuits operate. Some children may be falling behind because of their personal, social, and economic circumstances, or because of weaknesses in the teaching programmes they have previously received. It is well documented that substantial losses can occur over a summer vacation period where young children simply forget what they have learnt. Other children may be falling behind because of specific learning difficulties that are neuro-developmental in origin or learning differences like ADHD that have interrupted their ability to learn. All of these reasons can be considered distal causes to learning difficulties.

Proximal Causes

Proximal causes of learning difficulties are how the circuits themselves operate. Which circuits are working normally, and which circuits need some help? Put simply, we are interested in how the internal mechanisms of the machine are working together (proximal cause), as opposed to how the machine was built or how much use it has had (distal causes). Knowledge about how the circuits work is very valuable as it is from here that interventions can be developed. Interventions can then be personalised to meet the individual needs of the specific brain requiring help. Educational test batteries can be used to test a child's strengths and weaknesses, such as phonemic awareness, word recognition, non-word reading, digit-span and memory tests. Teachers should also closely monitor their children's performance in speaking, listening, reading, spelling, writing and mathematics. Within each cognitive operation, how are the sub-components working?

Figure 8.6 Causation Flowchart
The causation flowchart considers a child's learning difficulty in terms of it's environmental and genetic origins (distal causes), how the difficulty manifests and influences behaviour (promixal cause) and the resulting teaching programme that can help (intervention). As part of the flowchart, the intervention is strongly influenced by the proximal cause (how the brain is working), and this is affected by the distal causes (how the brain got to where it is).

Speaking Circuits: Assessment and Intervention

An informal assessment of children's speaking skills can be made by observing how they speak both to their peers and in class. By discussing their learning development with parents a complete understanding of their language skills can be formed. This assessment can then support the correct intervention. The following questions will help you separate out phonology, meaning and syntax related problems.

Dorsal 'Phonology' Circuit
Are they aware of sounds in words?
Can they recognise sounds at the beginning, middle or end of words?
Can they change (or manipulate) sounds in words?
How is their verbal short term memory?

Expressive 'Frontal' Area
Did they begin talking late? After the age of 2?
When they were 3, could their language be understood?
Do they have problems learning words and making conversations?
Do they have problems finding the appropriate word?

Receptive 'Temporal' Area
How are they at listening?
How is their comprehension?
How is their reading for meaning?

Syntax Dorsal and Ventral Circuits
Do they have problems with verbs?
Do they drop the –s off the end of present tense verbs?
Do they omit words during speaking?
Do they have problems putting together a sentence?

Intervention

Interventions should focus of the specific language difficulties the child is having. Usually, a speech and language therapist will be involved in carry out the intervention. Including parents in the intervention is also beneficial. Specific language impaired children will benefit from repeated practise of what was learnt in the classroom and with the speech pathologist.

Phonemic awareness training will be valuable for children who have difficulty isolating and manipulating sounds within language. There are a number of activities available to support phonemic and phonological development. Most of these are fun games involving matching or changing sounds. Often, the inclusion of activities with letters provides a more multi-sensory approach and supports memory as children learn. Also, playing with larger units of sound such as rhyming words is helpful for children as there is less loading on working memory.

Expressive and receptive language skills can be developed through games and activities that encourage role playing. Children can be given new and interesting words to learn on a daily basis. Mixed ability groups with role models or buddies (with stronger abilities) can be effective in the classroom for peer support and interaction.

Grammatical training, including the correct use of sentence structure and verbs may involve the modelling of appropriate linguistic forms, interwoven into everyday conversations so that new skills can be transferred into useful situations. Speaking and listening games and activities can be used to practise the correct use of grammar.

Reading Circuits: Assessment and Intervention

A number of opportunities arise for observing a child's reading skills and strategies during guided reading. Here, children are expected to make some errors or the reading level is too low. These errors can be used as clues as to how the two reading circuits are functioning together during reading. An understanding of a child's phonemic awareness will also be valuable in assessing their reading skills, as this should partially predict the capability of the dorsal reading circuit.

Dorsal 'Grapheme to Phoneme' Circuit

Does the child avoid a sounding out strategy when they meet an unknown word?

Are they poor at sounding out new words?

Do they fail to recognise the sounds of the various graphemes of English, including digraphs? (graphemes with more than one letter, but make one sound such as ch or igh)

Are they poor at blending sounds together?

Do they find tasks involving auditory memory difficult?

Do they sometimes swap words during reading with words that have a similar meaning?

Ventral 'Whole Word' Circuit

Are they poor at reading irregular words?

Do they make regularisation errors when reading irregular words? (i.e. sound out the word as if it was phonologically transparent)

Do they find tasks involving visual memory difficult?

Do they sometimes have problems reading high-frequency words?

Intervention

There are two circuits required for reading. Often, children with reading problems can show a relative strength in one circuit over the other. It is important to target the area of weakness when developing a reading intervention. This can be in the form of games and activities that build up the strength of the targeted circuit, or simply by guiding a child to a different reading strategy when they come across an unknown word during reading.

Some children will have difficulties sounding out words, despite the fact that they have received phonics instruction. Intervention needs to reinforce these grapheme-to-phoneme conversions, especially the ones they find difficult or have failed to learn. There are a number of multi-sensory techniques available for focused instruction. An effective approach is the use of colour-coded letter manipulatives. Colour-coding enables children to see different sound relationships and to see the patterns of letters in words (such as CVC). With moveable letters they can also see that by manipulating letters they are in fact manipulating sounds. Furthermore, by introducing word families they can also see that words with common patterns have common sounds.

Other children will have difficulty with rapidly accessing whole word configurations. The best way to build word recognition (in the letterbox) is extensive exposure to print. Children's stories often use repetition, rhythm and rhyme. Again this is a multi-sensory approach as these auditory features help the brain predict and access words. It will be important to find reading materials that encourage further reading. Reading words in context is the most effective way to learn new irregular words and to reinforce high frequency words. Meaning clues can be used to correct a regularisation error during guided reading. Alternatively, partial help can be offered by the teacher for sounding out the phonologically inconsistent component of the word.

Spelling Circuits: Assessment and Intervention

An analysis of children's spelling patterns during writing gives a powerful look into the relative strengths and weaknesses of the brain's spelling circuits. These patterns may also relate back to how the reading circuits operate, and how the phonology circuit operates in the speaking brain. Words that can't be read at flash can be used to test spelling strategies. For example, irregular words that can't be read at flash, should show an 'encoding' strategy (dorsal) during spelling. However, irregular words that can be read at flash, should show a 'direct recall' strategy (ventral) during spelling. Deviations from these patterns suggest one of the circuits is not working normally and supports intervention that focuses on that weakness.

Dorsal 'Encoding' Circuit

Do their misspellings show poor phonological accuracies?
Do they have problems using invented spellings (with phonological accuracy) in their writing?
Are their misspellings strange, showing letters in almost random patterns?

Ventral 'Direct Recall' Circuit

Do they have problems spelling irregular words?
Do they still have problems with spelling common high frequency words?
Do the sometimes make regularisation errors when spelling irregular words?
Do they have problems spelling homophones (such as their and there)?

Intervention

Children must have at least one grapheme for each of the 44 sounds so that they can invent spellings during writing. Encourage them to use these as a first try before using a dictionary. They should practise sounding the word out, then writing the letters that correspond to the sounds. There are a number of alternative spelling patterns for phonemes and children can be taught these with word family examples to show common patterns. Encoding skills will be strengthened by learning to read with phonics instruction. Children can also use the different spelling conventions and rules. A rule based approach simplifies spelling, in comparison to the complexities in English orthography of choosing a correct grapheme for a phoneme from multiple choices.

Children have to learn irregular words directly, perhaps with partial decoding support. Mnemonics can be used to teach irregular spellings. Mnemonics are verbal phrases that can be easily memorised to help with spelling patterns (for example, it is necessary to have 1 cream and 2 sugars in your coffee). Flash cards can also be helpful for teaching irregular features, such as silent letters, the rules of adding suffixes or irregular verb tenses.

Another bridging idea is introducing Latin and Greek derivatives. Prefix, suffixes and root words are phonologically friendly, as they are generally monosyllabic. Understanding their meaning provides additional clues during reading, spelling and writing. Word families involving prefix, suffix and root words can enable the rapid expansion of vocabulary.

Handwriting Circuit: Assessment and Intervention

Handwriting can be considered poor if it is difficult for people to read. Bad handwriting is sometimes referred to as 'spidery' or 'chicken scratches'. Slow handwriting is also a problem because children have to hold their ideas in working memory for longer periods of time before they can get them down.

Handwriting Circuit

Do they have messy handwriting? How legible is it?
Do they change the formation of letters across their handwriting?
Do they often mix up the order of letters?
Do they still make b and d reversal, even at an older age?
Is their handwriting slow?
Do they have to rest their head during writing? Is writing comfortable?
Are they reluctant to write? Do they give up easily?

Intervention

Sometimes children with difficulties hold their pencils in unconventional ways. Children should be first taught the dynamic tripod grip, where the pen is pinched between the forefinger and the ball of the thumb, supported by the middle finger. This position gives greatest control and minimises strain. Some children may require fine motor skill training, such as threading, cutting, pasting, or working with manipulatives. Often, targeted intervention will make a considerable difference. In others cases, handwriting remains hard despite further intervention.

One major challenge is that bright children with a faulty handwriting circuit may never manage to write fast enough to express their ideas on paper. If they do, they may do so at the expense of legibility. For these children a keyboard is an essential alternative and should be encouraged. Some handwriting skills are however a necessity as there are many times when handwriting is required. Subjects such as mathematics and science require handwriting, as well as everyday examples like completing forms.

Mathematics Circuits: Assessment and Intervention

The best approach with struggling learners of mathematics, like other processes, is to identify the areas of difficulty and to target intervention to these areas. Children with mathematics difficulties may also need extra help from someone and a personalised programme. The following questions can be used to assess the area of difficulty and for putting together an appropriate intervention.

Dorsal 'Quantitative' Circuit

Are they considerably better at addition than subtraction?
Do they have limited working memory for numbers?
Did they have difficulties with subitising when young?
Do they have problems with estimation of numbers, measurement or distance?
Can they count backwards from 50 easily? In multiples of 2 or 5?
Do they have problems navigating or using a map? Or poor sense of direction?
Do they have difficulty with the common use of money?
Do they seem to have little sense of number?

Ventral 'Memorised Calculation' Circuit

Do they have problems memorising tables?
Are they having problems with error free counting from memory?
Can they count forward easily in 1s, 2s, or 5s?
Can they do all of the above, but very slowly?

Frontal-Temporal 'Mathematical Language' Circuit

Do they have problems with the language of mathematics?
Do they have problems converting word equations into mathematical ones?

Intervention

Mathematics interventions can be taught with real-life examples to place teaching in the context of everyday life. Children can help with counting out change or with measuring the ingredients for a cake. In the classroom, they can help out by counting out papers to be passed around the classroom. Children with quantitative difficulties should practise estimating before solving an equation. The use of visual mathematics and manipulatives strong in multi-sensory learning can be an effective approach for demonstrating number patterns and concepts. For equation work, children will need reinforcement on the different ways to approach mathematical facts. The reciprocal relationships between addition and subtraction, as well as multiplication and division should be explained and demonstrated.

Children who have problems memorising number patterns, addition facts and multiplication tables may need drill type interventions. Again, a multi-sensory approach where number patterns are memorised to song my help with this. Flash cards may also be useful.

For those with language difficulties, teacher support may be needed to explain problems and ideas clearly. The use of graph paper has been recommended for children who have difficulty organising their ideas on paper. Children should review number and mathematical language. Teachers can demonstrate that numerical processes can be explained by different vocabulary that in fact carries the same meaning.

1. Insert Card.

2. Match question tiles to answers.

3. Turn over and check correct pattern matches.

Figure 8.7 Smart Tray System
The Smart Tray is a self-correcting activity system where the learner completes an activity and removes the card to see if the answer on the back matches. There are 13 sets of Accelerator cards that work with the Smart Tray, each designed to teach a specific component of the curriculum. The Smart Tray can be used for mainstream teaching, but is powerful as an intervention tool. Here the teacher can create an intervention programme based on the needs of the students.

Brain Care

A final mention should be made about taking care of the brain. Children need to drink lots of water as mild dehydration is shown to affect our ability to think. Sleep is also an important part of learning. Brain studies into sleep show the brain produces similar neural activities during the sleep state as in the wake state, in an effort to consolidate our memories. This process helps us to learn more the next time we are awake. A healthy regular diet is also important for learning. There is some soft evidence that a good diet of fish (or Omega 3) has positive effects on brain function. Caffeine, as taken in colas, decreases a child's alertness until they take another 'hit', so the general effect shows children are better off with a caffeine free lifestyle. Short exercise sessions have been shown to improve response times and may improve academic alertness. Overall, excise, healthy living and plenty of sleep are the best forms of brain care.

Conclusion

Numerous approaches to teaching from different fields have been included in this book. Much of this research comes from education and psychology. Working with children provides an insight into individual differences and which teaching techniques work. From a completely different perceptive, cognitive neuroscience allows the brain to be tested as a functional machine. Evolutionary psychology can explain where this machine has come from and the different areas that have been recycled for learning. Genetic research explains neurological diversity and the individual differences observed between children as they begin school. Finally, functional brain imaging gives us a peek inside the human brain as it learns and grows.

A better understanding of the neural underpinnings of education will help tailor pedagogical curricula towards a child's individual neuro-cognitive needs. The new science of education gives teachers a view into the brain to see how this remarkable machine is responding to instruction. Teachers can now know why their intuitions are right by understanding how the brain works. Furthermore, they won't need to make decisions based on their intuitions, as they can now begin to understand the science that is going on behind the behaviour.

Scaffolding supports children as they learn new concepts, enabling the brain to work at new learning thresholds. The zone of proximal development describes a level where children can extend themselves to learn new concepts with the help of scaffolding. Scaffolding comes from teacher led instruction, as well as reciprocal scaffolding when working in pairs or groups.

Technical scaffolding, such as the ipad, have expanded our brain's learning potential and reduced the age at which we can begin exploring and learning. Many new cultural revolutions exist for education and each will expand the ease, speed and capacity of learning. Such innovations will benefit children at a young age when their brains are incredibly plastic and open for reorganisation. New methods will be open for testing with brain imaging, so teachers will know exactly how and why they work.

The two-way interaction of neuroscience and education provides exciting opportunities for developing the best teaching approaches. Although, it is the job of the scientist to validate why certain techniques work and why some children struggle, this new science is still in its infancy. As it develops, it promises to offer more knowledge for teachers and accelerated learning for their children.

Appendix 1 - Phonics Progression

Phase Two:

Week	Letters	Word building examples	High Frequency Words
1	s – a – t – p -	sat tap pat	a as at
2	-i-	sit pit tip pip sip	is it
	n-/-n	pan pin tin tan nap	in an
	m-/-m	man mat map	am
	d-/-d	sad dip	dad did and
3	g-/-g	pig dig gas gap	
	-o-	pot top dog pop	got on not
	c-	cot cap cat cod	can
	k-	kid kit	
4	-ck	pack sack kick pick sick	
	-e-	pet ten net pen peg men neck	get
	-u-	run mug cup sun mud	mum up put (north)
	r-	rat rag ram rug rot rip rim	
	Tricky	to the (reading)	
5	h-	hot hut hop hit hat hum hug	had his him has
	b-	bad bag bed bug bus bat	big back but
	f-/-ff	fan fat fit fun fog puff huff	of if off
	l-/-ll	lap leg lit bell fill doll sell tell	let
	-ss	less hiss mess boss fuss kiss	
	Tricky	no go I into (reading)	
6	Revise		

Phase Three:

Week	Letters	Word building examples	High Frequency Words
1	j-	jam jab jug jog job jet	
	v-	van vet vat	
	w-	win wig wag web wax	will
	-x	mix fix box tax six	
	Tricky	to the no go I into (reading)	
2	y-	yes yet yap yell	
	z-	zip zigzag	
	-zz	buzz jazz	
	qu-	quit quiz quick quack	
3	ch-/-ch	chop chin chip chill check such rich much	
	sh-/-sh	ship shop shed shell fish cash rush	
	th-/-th	thin thick moth	that this them then with
	-ng	ring rang hang song wing king	

	-ng	long sing	
	Tricky	he she be (reading)	
4	-ai-	wait hail pain aim sail main tail rain bait	
	-ee-	feel weep feet jeep meet week deep keep	see
	-igh	high sigh light might night right sight fight tight	
	-oa-	coat load goat loaf road soap oak toad	
	Tricky	was (reading) no go (spelling)	
5	-oi-	oil boil coin coil join soil	
	-oo- (long)	zoo boot hoof zoom cool food root moon	too
	-oo- (short)	foot cook good book took wood wool hook	look
	-ow	owl cow how town	down now
	Tricky	my (reading)	
6	-ar	bar car bark card cart hard jar park	
	-air	air chair fair hair lair pair	
	-ear	ear dear fear hear gear near tear year rear	
	Tricky	you (reading)	
7	-er	germ perm term	
	-ur	fur burn burp curl hurt surf turn	
	-or	fork cork sort born worn fort torn short	for
	-ure	sure pure cure	
	Tricky	her they (reading)	
8-12	Revise	all are (reading)	

Progression Four:

Week	Letters	Word building examples	High Frequency Words
1	-st	nest best chest cost lost gust toast	just
	-nd	band land hand pond fond wind windmill	
	-mp	lamp damp camp limp chimp jump hump	
	-nt	tent dent hunt joint paint burnt	went
	-nk	bank thank sink link think bunk chunk	
	Tricky	said so (reading) he she we me be (spelling)	

2	-ft	gift lift shift tuft theft soft softest	
	-sk	ask task tusk husk desktop	
	-lt	tilt belt felt melt melting shelter	
	-lp	gulp helpdesk helper	help
	others	golf shelf (-lf) milk (-lk) kept (-pt) next (-xt)	
	Tricky	have you like come (reading) was you (spelling)	
3	tr-	trip tree train trash trail trend trust truck	
	dr-	drank drift droop drop drift driftwood	children
	gr-	grab green grip groan grunt grant grasp	
	cr-	cream creep crash crisp cramp crust crept	
	br-	brand bring brush brown brass	
	fr-	frog fresh frost frown freshness	from
	Tricky	were there little one (reading) they all are (spelling)	
4	bl-	bleed blend blink blank blast	
	fl-	flag flair float floating	
	gl-	glad glass glint	
	pl-	plan plum plump	
	cl-	clamp clown clear	
	sl-	slept slant	
	Tricky	do when out what (reading) my her (spelling)	
5	sp-	spot spin spoil spoon sport speech spend	
	st-	stop step steep start star stair stand stamp	
	tw-	twin twist twisting	
	sm-	smell smart smear	
	others	printer (pr) scoop (sc) skunk (sk) sniff (sn)	
6	-nch	bench drench trench punch crunch lunchbox	it's
	scr-	scrunch scrap	
	shr-	shrink	
	str-	strap string street	
	thr-	thrust thrush thrill	

Progression Five:

Week	Letters	Word building examples	High Frequency Words
1	-ay	play may say stray clay spray tray	day
	-ou-	out cloud scout found proud sprout	about house
	-ie	pie lie tie die cried tried spied fried	
	-ea-	sea seat meat treat heap least repeat	
	Tricky	oh their (reading) said so (spelling)	
2	-oy	boy toy joy oyster destroy enjoy royal	
	-ir	girl sir bird shirt skirt birth third first	
	-ue	blue clue glue true issue tissue venue	
	-aw	paw raw claw jaw lawn yawn law	saw
	Tricky	people Mr. Mrs. (reading) have like (spelling)	
3	wh-	when which wheel whisper	
	ph-	phonics dolphin elephant alphabet	
	-ew	new few stew blew chew grew drew screw	
	-oe	toe hoe doe foe woe goes tomatoes	
	-au-	haul launch haunted August author	
	Tricky	looked called (reading) some come (spelling	
4	a-e	take game race snake	came made make
	e-e	these even theme gene scene complete	
	i-e	like pine ripe shine slide prize nice	time
	o-e	bone pole home alone those stone woke	
	u-e	June flute prune rude rule	
	/zh/	treasure vision television	

	/zh/ -s- -ge	treasure vision television pleasure leisure visual measure usual casual beige	
	Tricky	asked (reading) were there (spelling)	
5	Alternative pronunciations of graphemes: c g ch y		by
	Tricky	water where who again thought through (reading) little (spelling)	put (south)
6	Alternative pronunciations of graphemes: a i o u		old
	Tricky	work mouse many laughed because (reading) one do out (spelling)	
7	Alternative pronunciations of graphemes: ea ie er ow ou		
	Tricky	different any eyes friends once please (reading) when what (spelling)	
8-30	Alternative spelling of phonemes: /c/ /ch/ /f/ /j/ /m/ /n/ /ng/ /r/ /s/ /sh/ /v/ /w/ /e/ /i/ /o/ /u/ /ai/ /ee/ /igh/ /oa/ /oo/ /oo/ /ar/ /or/ /ur/ /ow/ /oi/ /ear/ /air/ /ure/ /er/		very your
	Tricky	oh their people Mr. Mrs. looked called asked (spelling)	here

Appendix 2 - Mathematical Stages Model

Stage	Goals	Number Level	Key Vocabulary	Questions
1	development of children's early awareness of quantity and the use of the language of number	Introduction of numbers	more, less, few, more than, less than, fewer, fewer than, number, one, many, lots, lots of, a few, a lot, order, count, pattern, same, next, one, two, three...	How many? Which/what number...? What does this number tell us?
2	develop knowledge and use of the number sequence from one to five, recognition of the numerals 1 to 5, counting up to five objects and subitising (instantly recognising without counting) sets of one, two and three objects	1-5	number, order, count, after, one, two, three, four, five, forwards, backwards, straight, curved, least, fewer, amount, the same as	What number comes next? How many..? What does the number look like?
3	number recognition from 1 to 10 in terms of sequencing and object counting	1-10	number, order, count, one, two, three, four, five, six, seven, eight, nine, ten, forwards, backwards, next, before, straight, curved, more, less, few, more than, fewer, fewer than, amount, same as	How many altogether? What number comes next? How many...? What does the number look like?
4	the range of numbers from 0 to 20. Children should be able to count up to ten objects in any arrangement. As children begin to partition and combine sets to remove objects from sets they will develop early stages of addition and subtraction.	0-20	number, order, count, zero, eleven, twelve, thirteen, fourteen, fifteen, sixteen, seventeen, eighteen, nineteen, twenty, first, second, third, forwards, backwards, next, before, between, pattern, sequence, total, more, less, more than, less than, fewer, fewer than, amount, one more, one less, estimate, guess, before, after	How many left? How many altogether? What number comes next? How many...?
5	the number range which children can confidently use is extended to 50. Children can also start exploring different sequence of numbers when they count from zero in twos, fives and tens. Counting skills can be extended to enable them to estimate, count and compare sets of up to 20 objects. Addition and subtraction are further developed as children partition and combine sets and count on and back.	0-50	number, order, count, pattern, zero, twenty-one, twenty-two..., twenty-nine, ten, twenty, thirty, forty, fifty, forwards, backwards, next, before, between, sequence, first, second, third, fourth, fifth... What number comes next? How many...? What order...?, estimate, about, more, less, most, least, more than, less than, amount, count on, count back, put together, add together, total, take away	What order...? What number comes next? How many...? How many altogether? How many are left?
6	extends the number range up to 100. Children will become more secure counting forwards and backwards in twos, fives and tens.	0-100	number, count, pattern, forwards, backwards, next, before, between, sequence, number, names to 100, multiple, Count in twos, fives, tens., count on, count back, order, add together, add, total, take away, subtract, difference	What is the difference between? How many altogether? How many are left? What number comes next? What is the number before...?

Footnotes

1. Dehaene, 2009.
2. Milne, 2005.
3. Dehaene, 2009.
4. Castro-Caldas et al., 1998; Castro-Caldas et al., 1999.
5. Dehaene-Lambertz et al., 2009.
6. Leroy et al., 2011.
7. Friederici, 2012.
8. Saur et al., 2008.
9. Hagoort, 2005.
10. Hickok and Poeppel, 2007.
11. Ravizza, 2008.
12. Hickok and Poeppel, 2007.
13. Every Child a Talker, 2010.
14. Milne, 2005.
15. Ishai et al., 2000.
16. Dehaene, 2009.
17. Warrington and Shallice, 1980.
18. Letters and Sounds, 2007.
19. Rose, 2006; Letters and Sounds, 2007.
20. Roux et al., 2009.
21. Letters and Sounds, 2007.
22. Corballis and Beale, 1976.
23. Goodale and Milner, 1992.
24. Joseph, 2000.
25. Rapp and Dufor, 2011.
26. Simon and Vaishnavi, 1996.
27. Ward, Sagiv and Butterworth, 2009.
28. Dehaene and Cohen, 1997.
29. Numbers and Patterns: Laying Foundations in Mathematics, 2009.
30. Grigorenko, 2003; Fisher and Francks, 2006; Galaburda et al., 2006.
31. Galaburda et al., 1985.
32. Silani et al., 2005.
33. Habib, 2003.
34. Sherman, Galaburda & Geschwind, 1985.
35. Milne and Santos, 2005.

36. Paulesu et al., 2001.
37. Salani et al., 2005.
38. Shaywitz et al., 1998; Simos et al., 2002; Temple et al., 2003; Aylward et al., 2003.
39. Milne, Nicholson and Corballis, 2003.
40. Nicolson and Fawcett, 2011.
41. Siok et al., 2004.
42. Milne, Hamm, Kirk and Corballis, 2003.
43. Butterworth, 2012.
44. Dale & Cole, 1991.
45. Robinson, 1991.
46. Hugdalh et al., 2004.
47. Galaburda, Menard and Rosen, 1994.
48. Alloway, 2007.
49. Stein, 2001.
50. Nicholson, Fawcett and Dean, 2001.
51. Ramus 2004.
52. Ramus 2004.
53. Schneider & Eisenberg, 2006.
54. Swanson et al., 2000.
55. Racine et al., 2008.
56. Montes & Halterman, 2007.
57. Volkmar, State & Klin, 2009.
58. Simos et al., 2002.
59. Milne, Syngeniotis, Jackson and Corballis, 2002; Shaywitz et al., 1998.
60. West, 1997.
61. Hartman, 2002.
62. Kujala et al., 2001.
63. Rose, 2006.

Glossary

Accelerated learning: Teaching systems for speeding up and enhancing the learning experience.

Acquired dyslexia: When a person loses reading ability as a result of brain damage.

Addition: a mathematical operation involved with combining objects into a larger collection.

ADHD: attention deficit hyperactivity disorder is a problem with inattentiveness, overactivity, impulsivity, or a combination.

Alphabet principle: learning the shapes and names of the letters of the alphabet.

Analogy: relating something known to something new. In reading and spelling, using knowledge of one word to read and spell other words, e.g. shell = /sh/ as in shoe and /ell/ as in bell.

Analytic phonics: teaching children how to decode new words by breaking up words that they already know and finding similarities.

Antonyms: words that are opposites, e.g. near is an antonym for far.

Arithmetic: a branch of mathematics involved with computation.

Asperger's: is an autistic spectrum disorder characterised by difficulties with the development of social interaction without problems in linguistic and cognitive development.

Asymmetrical: when one side is bigger than the other side, e.g. the human brain shows a left hemisphere asymmetry, where the left side of the brain is bigger than the right.

Auditory discrimination: the ability to distinguish between different sounds.

Autism: is a disorder of neural origin that affects the brain's normal development of social interaction and communication.

Balanced literacy: a method of teaching that places equal weighting on synthetic phonics, analytic phonics, and whole language.

Base ten: the decimal numeral system.

Behavioural research: research that involves measuring behaviour and does not look at brain processing.

Blended learning: the mixing of learning environments, including face-to-face and computer based technologies.

Blending: bringing sounds together, e.g. blend these sounds together, /h/a/n/d.

Broca's area: a region in the frontal lobe that is involved in speech production.

Calculation: the process of transforming an input into an outcome.

Camouflage learning: disguising a learning activity as a game.

Cerebellum: a separate structure that sits behind the cerebrum and is involved with motor control.

Cerebrum: the largest and most developed part of the human brain.

Chinese reading: a style of reading where words are learnt directly through rote memorisation.

Common core deficits: overlapping problems seen in many children with learning differences including language, phonology and coordination difficulties.

Co-morbidity: the presence of one or more disorders in addition to a primary disorder.

Compensation: occurs when areas of the brain rewire and engage in the processes of a damaged or malfunctioning area.

Connectionism: considering the brain as a complex interconnection of neurons that form a learning system.

Contractions: words where letters have been removed and replaced with an appostrophy, effectively shortening the word.

Corpus callosum: a thick bundle of nerves that connects the left and right hemispheres of the brain.

Cortex: the outer layer of the cerebrum.

Counting: the action of finding the number of elements in a finite set.

CVC: a spelling pattern referring to a consonant-vowel-consonant sequence of letters. It is associated with the short vowel sound, e.g. c/a/t, d/o/g, m/a/n, h/i/d.

Decimals: a series of nested tenths to represent quantities smaller than one unit.

Decodeable books: books that are written with phonologically transparent letter patterns. Books with decodeable patterns can be linked into a phonics progression.

Decoding: conversion from letter to sound (a dorsal reading circuit process).

Deleting: removing a sound within a word, e.g. say plate without the /p/ sound.

Developmental delay: when cognitive development occurs at a slower rate than normal.

Developmental dyslexia: a genetic condition marked by severe reading difficulties despite adequate instruction and intelligence.

Diffuser tensor imaging: a magnetic resonance imaging method that maps the diffusion process of water molecules to give microscopic details of tissue architecture.

Direct access: a way of getting straight to a word's pronunciation and meaning from visual input (a ventral reading circuit process).

Direct recall: a way of directly accessing the visual properties of a whole word from a pronunciation (a ventral spelling circuit process).

Distal causes: a higher level or ultimate cause.

Diversity: the existence of many unique learners in the classroom.

Division: a mathematical operation involved with seeing how many times a group is represented in a larger set.

DNA: deoxyribonucleic acid that contains genetic instructions.

Dorsal circuit: an upper pathway in charge of computing relationships.

Dorsal stream: an upper pathway to the parietal lobe involved in the guidance of actions and recognising where objects are in space.

Dyscalculia: a condition that affects the ability to acquire number and arithmetic skills despite adequate instruction and intelligence.

Dys-constellation: a group of specific learning difficulties with common genetic and neuro-biological origins.

Dyseidetic: a type of spelling difficulty showing difficulty in memorising whole word forms.

Dysgraphia: a condition that affects the ability to acquire handwriting skills despite adequate instruction and intelligence.

Dyslexia: a condition marked by severe reading and spelling difficulties.

Dysorthographia: a condition that affects the ability to acquire spelling skills despite adequate instruction and intelligence.

Dysphonetic: a type of spelling difficulty showing difficulty in encoding words.

Dyspraxia: a condition affecting motor learning and balance. Dyspraxics show poor coordination skills and may have problems with eye-hand coordination.

Ectopia: a tiny bundle of brain cells that disrupts the cell migration process during the third trimester.

Electroencephalography (EEG): a method for measuring brain wave patterns that uses electrodes placed on the scalp.

Encoding: conversion from sound to letter (a dorsal spelling circuit process).

Exception words: words that don't follow the letter/sound relationships of English. Sometimes called irregular or tricky words.

Exner's area: an area in the frontal lobe above Broca's area that is involved in handwriting.

Fluency: having command of reading. Reading easily and effortlessly.

Fovea: a part of the eye responsible for sharp central vision.

Fractions: a part of a whole.

Frontal lobes: an area in the front of the brain involved in speech production, working memory, attention and reward.

Functional magnetic resonance imaging (fMRI): a method for measuring brain activation patterns by placing the brain inside a large magnetic field.

Garden-variety poor reader: a reader who has underdeveloped reading circuits because of insufficient instruction or developmental delay.

Generation effect: an effect that improves learning (memory) when you actually create something for yourself (learning by doing).

Genes: a molecular unit of heredity.

Grapheme: The written representation of a sound, which may consist of one or more letters.

Grapheme-to-phoneme conversion: the computation involved with sounding out a word (working from letter to sound).

Guided reading: small group reading instruction where the readers are grouped according to their reading ability. The teacher sets the purpose for reading and works intensively with the group to support the reading of a carefully selected text.

Hetrophonic vowels: vowel digraphs that make more than one sound, e.g. /oo/ as in good and goose and /ow/ as in cow and tow.

High frequency words: the most commonly seen and used words, e.g. come, going, up, look.

Homonyms: words that sound alike but have different meanings, e.g. blue and blew.

Homophones: words that sound the same.

Illiteracy: a lack of schooling and thus the inability to read and write.

Implicit learning: learning something without consciously being aware of learning it.

Inclusion: creating environments that include all types of learners.

Independent learning: providing texts at an appropriate level that can be read without guided or shared support from teachers.

Informal learning: learning that is occurring on an ongoing basis and occurring independently from direct instruction.

Intervention: a programme designed to modify the pattern of reading behaviour.

Inventive spelling: when children make up the spelling of a word they don't know based on sound-letter relationships, often producing phonologically acceptable misspelling.

IQ discrepancy: a method for diagnosing developmental dyslexic based on a discrepancy between the sub-scales of intelligence tests, e.g. superior performance at block design while low average for decoding.

Irlen syndrome: a visual perceptual disorder affecting reading and writing activities. Also referred to as Scotopic Sensitivity Syndrome and Visual Stress.

Irregular verbs: verbs that do not follow normal rules of past and present, such as go – went.

Irregular words: words that don't follow the letter/sound relationships of English. Sometimes called exception or tricky words.

Isolating: focusing on one sound in a word, e.g. what is the first, middle or last sound in cat?

Kinaesthetic: learning which uses touch and movement.

Language gap: the proficiency and vocabulary distance between socioeconomic groups.

Latent variable: the underlying variable that you want to measure.

Learning delay: when a child does not reach their developmental milestones in expected times.

Lesion: an abnormality in brain tissue caused by disease or injury.

Letterbox: an area in the back of the brain in charge of storing whole word forms. Also referred to as the visual word form area.

Lexicalisation: the process of storing a representation of a visual word form (like taking a snapshot of a new word).

Literacy: the ability to read, write and think about the written word.

Logographic stage: an early stage of reading development where words are memorised from their visual properties or shapes.

Low frequency words: words that are not seen very often or used very much.

Magnetoencephalography: a brain-imaging technique that records magnetic fields produced by electrical currents.

Magnocellular Cells: large sized neurons primarily concerned with visual perception.

Manipulatives: an object designed so the learner can perceive a concept by manipulating it.

Matching: comparing sounds between two words, e.g. do big and bat start with the same sound?

Matthew effect: an effect where the poor learners get worse due to low confidence, motivation and resource allocation.

Microscopic: so small as to only be visible with a microscope.

Millisecond (msec): one thousandth of a second.

Mirror writing: writing in the reverse direction.

Mnemonic: a method of aiding the memory to learn a particular spelling, e.g. there is a piece of pie.

Modality: relating to a sensory mode, e.g. visual, auditory or kinaesthetic modalities.

Module: an independent unit within the brain that is specialised for a particular type of processing or analysis.

Monosyllabic: containing only one syllable.

Morpheme: the smallest unit of meaning. Prefixes and suffixes are morphemes.

Multiplication: a mathematical operation involved with scaling one number by another.

Multisensory learning: a method of teaching that focuses on engaging the different senses: auditory, visual and kinaesthetic.

Nonsense words: made up words (that are not in the dictionary) used to test how children go about sounding out new words. Sometimes called non-words or pseudo-words.

Number grid: a chart of numbers typically from 1 to 100 which represents ten rows of numbers according to base ten.

Number line: a line of numbers with ordinal numbers marked on it.

Number track: a series of number cells with ordinal numbers presented in them.

Occipital lobes: an area at the back of the brain involved with visual processing.

Onset: the initial consonant or consonant cluster of a syllable, e.g. c-at, br-ick.

Ordinality: using numbers to define the sequence of an item.

Orthography: a standardised system for using a particular writing system.

Orthography: correct or conventional spelling.

Palindrome: a word or line that reads the same backwards as forwards, e.g. dad.

Parietal lobes: an area at the top back of the brain involved with spatial processing and number concepts.

Pedagogy: the science of education as the correct use of instructional strategies.

Percentages: a number or ratio as a fraction of one hundred.

Personalised learning: tailoring of pedagogy, curriculum and learning environments to meet the needs of the individual learner.

Phoneme: the smallest unit of sound in a written word, e.g. /c/-/a/-/t/.

Phonemic awareness: an understanding that words are made up of small units of sounds called phonemes. It is also the ability to consciously manipulate and hear the individual phonemes in words.

Phonetian reading: a style of reading where words are read letter-by-letter or sounded out.

Phonics progression: a sequential method of introducing letter patterns to emergent readers, where new letters build on knowledge previously learnt so that all letters are decodeable.

Phonics: a systematic instructional method for teaching the relationships between letters and sounds.

Phonological assembly: the process where words can be constructed or manipulated based on their letter to sound relationships.

Phonological awareness: an awareness of various speech sounds such as rhyme, syllables and individual phonemes.

Phonological dyslexia: a type of dyslexia where the sounding out mechanism appears deficient (dorsal grapheme-to-phoneme circuit), while the word accessing mechanism remains intact (ventral 'direct access' circuit).

Phonologically accurate misspellings: spelling mistakes that follow the rules of letter/sound relationships.

Phonologically inaccurate misspellings: spelling mistakes that do not follow the rules of letter/sound relationships.

Phonology: the systematic organisation of sounds in language.

Place value: the numerical value a digit has by virtue of its position in a number.

Plasticity: changing in the structure, function and organisation of neurons.

Polysyllabic: a word that contains more than one syllable.

Positron emission topography: a brain-imaging method that develops 3 dimensional images of functional brain activity by recording a tracer.

Precocious readers: children with premature development of their reading circuits.

Prefrontal cortex: the front part of the frontal lobe involved in planning, personality, decision making and monitoring social behaviour.

Prevention: designing inclusive early reading programmes to stop or minimise reading failure.

Proximal causes: an event which is closest to or immediately responsible for causing an observed result.

Pseudo-words: made up of words (that are not in the dictionary) used to test how children go about sounding out new words. Sometimes called non-words or nonsense-words.

Reading circuits: a series of circuits in the left brain that are engaged during reading.

Reading efficacy: refers to the belief that one can be successful at reading.

Reading pattern: the observed pattern of a reader in terms of sounding out (dorsal circuit) and word access (ventral circuit) skills.

Reading variability: the range of individual differences in reading patterns.

Remediation: programmes designed to help children who are slow readers or who are experiencing difficulty acquiring reading skills.

Retina: a light sensitive tissue on the inner lining of the eye.

Rhyme: a word rhymes with another word when it has a similar sound in its final syllable, e.g. rode and toad.

Rime: a unit of sound composed of the vowel and any following consonants within a syllable, e.g. –at as in cat, mat or bat.

Scaffolding: temporary support provided by teachers to enable independent learning.

Scotopic sensitivity syndrome: a visual perceptual disorder affecting reading and writing activities. Also referred to as Irlen Syndrome and Visual Stress.

Segmenting: separating sounds in a word, e.g. what are the separate sounds in dog?

Semantic: relating to meaning in language.

Semantically incongruent: where the meaning is out of place, despite being grammatically correct.

Shared reading: the teacher models the reading process by reading to the pupils. The text may be at a level too difficult to be read independently. Pupils join in with the reading and are later encouraged to re-read all or part of the text.

Sight words: high frequency words that are learnt directly. Often these are function words (e.g. of, the, that) that lack simple semantic association or are irregular and lack phonological transparency.

Silent letters: letters that make no sound in the pronunciation of words.

Spatial resolution: the clarity of knowing exactly where a change is occurring in the brain.

Specific language impairment: a condition affecting oral language development despite adequate instruction and intelligence.

Spelling log: a word list of spelling patterns to be learnt.

Statistical validity: whether something is statistically sound and is measuring what it is supposed to measure, i.e. the latent variable.

Subitising: instantly recognising the number of objects in a small group without actually counting them.

Substituting: replacing a sound within a word, e.g. change the first sound in cat to an /m/ sound.

Subtraction: a mathematical operation involved with removing objects from a collection to make a smaller one.

Suffix: a letter or group of letters that can be added to the end of a word to alter its meaning.

Superior temporal gyrus: part of the temporal lobe that contains the primary auditory cortex which is responsible for processing sounds.

Surface dyslexia: a type of dyslexia where the word accessing mechanism appears deficient (ventral circuit), while the decoding mechanism remains intact (dorsal circuit).

Syllable: a part of a word that contains a single vowel sound and is said as one unit, e.g. looking has two syllables, cat has one syllable.

Symmetrical: a structure where the parts are an equal shape and size.

Synonyms: a word with the same or a very similar meaning to another, e.g. a synonym for loud is noisy.

Synthetic phonics: an instructional method that explicitly teaches the 44 phonemes of the English language and their corresponding graphemes.

Temporal lobes: an area along the bottom of the brain involved with auditory perception, long term memories, comprehension, face recognition, letter and word identification.

Temporal resolution: the clarity of knowing exactly when a change is occurring within the brain.

Thalamus: a structure within the brain that relays sensory and motor signals to the brain.

Transcranial magnetic stimulation (TMS): a brain imaging methodology where the cortex is temporarily disrupted through magnetic stimulation.

Tricky words: words that don't follow the letter/sound relationships of English. Sometimes called exception or irregular words.

Ventral circuit: a lower pathway typically involved with direct access or recall of a memorised fact.

Ventral stream: a lower pathway to the temporal lobe involved in recognising what an object is.

Verbal fluency: the number of words a child knows and uses during oral expression.

Visual streams: two pathways used in visual processing that recognise objects in terms of what and where.

Visual stress: a visual perceptual disorder affecting reading and writing activities. Also referred to as Scotopic Sensitivity Syndrome and Irlen Syndrome.

Visual word form area: an area in the back of the brain in charge of storing whole word forms. Also referred to as the letterbox.

Wernicke's area: an area at the back of the superior temporal gyrus that is involved with understanding written and spoken language.

Whole language: a technique for teaching new words in the context of real reading. An emphasis is placed on meaning, syntax and sight vocabulary.

Word families: families of words that contains analogous properties, e.g. cat, bat, and sat make an –at rime word family.

References

Alloway, T.P. 2007. Working memory, reading and mathematical skills in children with developmental coordination disorder. *Journal of Experimental Child Psychology*, 96, 1, 20-36.

Ardila, A., Rosselli, M. 2002. Acalculia and dyscalculia. *Neuropsychological Review*, 12, 4, 179-231.

Aylward, E.H., Richards, T.L., Berninger, V.W., Nagy, W.E., Field, K.M., Grimme, A.C., Richards, A.L., Tomson, J.B. & Cramer, S.C. 2003. *Instructional treatment associated with changes in brain activation in children with dyslexia.* Neurology, 61, 212-219

Beaulieu, C. Plewes, C. Paulson, L.A., Roy, D. Snook, L., Concha, L. & Phillips, L. 2005. Imaging brain connectivity in children with diverse reading ability, Neuroimage, 25 (4), 1266-1271.

Berninger, V.W. & May M.O. 2011. Evidence-based diagnosis and treatment for specific learning disabilities involving impairments in written and/or oral language. *Journal of Learning Disabilities,* 44, 2, 167-183.

Binder, J.R., Frost, J.A., Hammeke, T.A., Bellowan, P.S., Springer, J.A., Kaufman, J.N., & Possing, E.T. 2000. Human temporal lobe activation by speech and nonspeech sounds. *Cerebral Cortex*, 10, 5, 512-528.

Binder, J.R., McKiernan, K.A., Parsons, M.E., Westbury, C.F., Possing, E.T., Kaufman, J.N. & Buchanan, L. 2003. Neural correlates of lexical access during visual word recognition. *Journal of Cognitive Neuroscience*, 15, 3, 372-393.

Binder, J.R., Medler, D.A., Westbury, C.F., Liebenthal, E. & Buchanan, L. 2006. Tuning of the human left fusiform gyrus to sublexical orthographic structure. *Neuroimage*, 33, 2, 739-748.

Bishop, D.V., Snowling, M.J. 2004. Developmental dyslexia and specific language impairment: same or different? *Psychological Bulletin* 130, 6, 858-886.

Bradley, L. & Bryant, P. 1983. Categorizing sounds and learning to read: A causal connection. *Nature*, 30, 419-421.

Butterworth, B. 1999. *The Mathematical Brain*. Macmillan, London, England.

Butterworth, B. 2010. Foundational numerical capacities and the origins of dyscalculia. *Trends in Cognitive Sciences*, 14, 12, 534-541.

Castro-Caldas, A., Miranda, P.C., Carmo, I., Reis, A., Leote, F., Ribeiro, C., & Ducla-Soares, E. 1999. Influence of learning to read and write on the morphology of the corpus callosum. *European Journal of Neurology*, 6, 1, 23-28.

Castro-Caldas, A., Petersson, K.M., Reis, A., Stone-Elander, S. & Ingvar, M. 1998. The illiterate brain: Learning to read and write during childhood influences the functional organization of the adult brain. *Brain*, 121, 6, 1053-1063.

Cohen, L., Jobert, A., Le Bihan, D. & Dehaene, S. 2004. Distinct unimodal and multimodal regions for word processing in the left temporal cortex. *Neuroimage*, 23, 4, 1256-1270.

Coltheart, M., Rastle, K., Perry, C., Langdon, R. & Ziegler, J.C. 2001. DRC: A dual route cascaded model of visual word recognition and reading aloud. *Psychological Review*, 108, 1, 204-256.

Corballis, M.C. & Beale, I.L. (1976). The psychology of left and right. New York: Erlbaum.

Corballis, M.C., Macadie, L., Crotty, A. & Beale, I.L. 1985. The naming of disoriented letters by normal and reading-disabled children. *Journal of Child Psychology and Psychiatry*, 26, 6, 929-938.

Cornell, J. 1985. Spontaneous mirror-writing in children. *Canadian Journal of Experimental Psychology*, 39, 174-179.

Dale, P. S., & Cole, K. N. 1991. What's normal? Specific language impairment in an individual differences perspective. *Language, Speech and Hearing Services in Schools*, 22, 80–83.

Dehaene, S. 1997. The Number Sense. Oxford University Press, Oxford, England.

Dehaene, S. 2009. Reading in the Brain. Penguin Group, New York.

Dehaene, S., Cohne, L., Sigman, M. & Vinckier, F. 2005. The neural code for written words: A proposal. *Trends in Cognitive Neuroscience*, 9, 7, 335-341.

Dehaene, S., Jobert, A., Naccache, L., Ciuciu, P., Poline, J.B., Le Bihan, D. & Cohen, L. 2004. Letter binding and invariant recognition of masked words in the fusiform gyrus. *Neuro Report*, 13, 3, 321-325.

Dehaene, S., Piazza, M., Pinel, P. & Cohen, L. 2003. Three parietal circuits for number processing. *Cognitive Neuropsychology*, 20, 487-506.

Dehaene-Lambertz, G., Montavont, A., Jobert, A., Allirol, L., Hertz-Pannier & Dehaene, S. 2010. Language or music, mother or Mozart? Structural and environmental influences on infants' language networks. *Brain & Language*, 114 (2), 53-65.

Dehaneae, S. & Cohen, L. 1997. Cerebral pathways for calculation: double dissociation between rote verbal and quantitative knowledge of arithmetic. *Cortex*, 33, 2, 219-250.

DFES (2007). Letters and Sounds: Principles and Practice of High Quality Phonics. *Primary National Strategy*, England.

DFES (2009). Numbers and Patterns: Laying Foundations in Mathematics. *Primary National Strategy*. England.

Ehri, L.C., Nunes, S.R., Stahl, S.A. & Willows, D.M.M. 2001. Systematic phonics instruction helps students learn to read: Evidence from the National Reading Panel's meta-analysis. *Review of Educational Research*, 71, 393-447.

Fiebach, C.J., Friederici, A.D., Muller, K. & von Cramon, D.Y. 2002. fMRI evidence for dual routes to the mental lexicon in the visual word recognition. *Journal of Cognitive Neuroscience*, 14, 1, 11-23.

Fisher, S.E. & Francks, C. 2006. Genes, cognition and dyslexia: Learning to read the genome. *Trends in Cognitive Sciences*, 10, 6, 250-257.

Fox, M.D., Corbetta, M., Snyder, A.Z., Vincent, J.L. & Raichle, M.E. 2006. Spontaneous neuronal activity distinguishes human dorsal and ventral attention systems. *Proceedings of the National Academy of Sciences*, 103, 26, 10046-10051.

Frey, S., Campbell, J.S.W., Pike, G.B., & Petrides, M. 2008. Dissociating the human language pathways with high angular resolution diffusion fiber tractography. *The Journal of Neuroscience*, 28 (45), 11435-11444.

Friederici, A.D. 2012. Language development and the ontogeny of the dorsal pathway. *Frontiers in Evolutionary Neuroscience*, 4, 3, 1-7.

Galaburda, A.M. & Kember, T.L. 1979. Cytoarchitectonic abnormalities in developmental dyslexia: a case study. *Annals of Neurology*, 6, 94-100.

Galaburda, A.M. & Livingstone, M. 1993. Evidence for a magnocellular deficit in developmental dyslexia. In Tallal, P., Galaburda, A.M., Llinas, R. & Von Euler, C. (Eds). Temporal information processing in the nervous system: Special reference to dyslexia and dysphasia (pp. 70-82). New York: New York Academy of Sciences.

Galaburda, A.M., LoTurco, J., Ramus, F., Fitch, R.H. & Rosen, G.D. 2006. From genes to behavior in developmental dyslexia. *Nature Neuroscience*, 9, 10, 1213-1217.

Galaburda, A.M., Menard, M.T. & Rosen, G.D. 1994. Evidence for aberrant auditory anatomy in developmental dyslexia. *Proceedings of the National Academy of Sciences*, 91, 17, 8010-8013.

Galaburda, A.M., Sherman, G.F., Rosen, G.D., Aboitiz, F. & Geschwind, N. 1985. Developmental dyslexia: Four consecutive patients with cortical anomalies. *Annals of Neurology*, 18, 2, 222-233.

Goodale, M.A. & Milner, A.D. 1992. Separate visual pathways for perception and action. *Trends in Neuroscience*, 15, 1, 20-25.

Goswami, U. 1986. Children's use of analogy in learning to read. A developmental study. *Journal of Experimental Child Psychology*, 42, 73-83.

Grigorenko, E.L. 2003. The first candidate gene for dyslexia: Turning the page of a new chapter of research. *Proceedings of the National Academy of Sciences*, 100, 20, 11190-11192.

Habib, M. 2003. La dyslexie a livre ouvert. Marseille, France: RESODYS.

Hagoort, P. 2005. On Broca, brain and binding: a new framework. *Trends in Cognitive Sciences*, 9, 9, 416-423.

Hannula-Jouppi, K., Kaminen-Ahola, N., Taipale, M., Eklund, R., Nopola-Hemmi, J., Kaariainen, H. & Kere, J. 2005. The axon guidance receptor gene ROBO1 is a candidate gene for developmental dyslexia. PLoS Genetics, 1, 4, e50.

Hartman, H. 2002. Scaffolding & cooperative learning. *Human Learning and Instruction*, New York: City College of City University New York, 23-69.

Hickok, G. & Poeppel, D. 2007. The cortical organisation of speech. *Nature Neuroscience*, 8, 393-402.

Hugdahl, K., Gundersen, H., Brekke, L., Thomsen, T., Rimol, L.M., Ersland, L. & Niomi, J. 2004. fMRI brain activation in a finnish family with specific language impairment compared with a normal control group. *Journal of Speech, Language and Hearing*, 47, 1, 162-172.

Ishai, A., Ungerleider, L.G., Martin, A. & Haxby, J.V. 2000. The representation of objects in the human occipital and temporal cortex. *Journal of Cognitive Neuroscience*, 12, 2, 35-51.

Ishai, A., Ungerleider, L.G., Martin, A., Schouten, J.L. & Haxby, J.V. 1999. Distributed representations of objects in the human ventral visual pathway. *Proceedings of the National Academy of Sciences*, 96, 16, 9379-9384.

Jenner, A.R., Rosen, G.D. & Galaburda, A.M. 1999. Neuronal asymmetries in primary visual cortex of dyslexic and nondyslexic brains. *Annals of Neurology*, 46, 189-196.

Joseph, R. 2000. Neuropsychiatry, Neuropsychology, Clinical Neuroscience. Academic press. New York.

Kirby, A., Davies, R. & Bryant, A. 2005. Do teachers know more about specific learning difficulties than general practitioners? *British Journal of Special Education*, 32, 3, 122-126.

Kroger, J.K. Nystrom, L.E., Cohn, J.D., Johnson-Laird, P.N. 2008. Distinct neural substrates for deductive and mathematical processing. *Brain Research*, 1243, 86-103.

Kujala, T., Karma, K., Cerponiene, R., Belitz, S., Turkkila, P., Tervanieme, M & Naatanen, R. 2001. Plastic neural changes and reading improvement caused by audiovisual training in reading impaired children. *Proceedings of the National Academy of Science*, 98, 18, 10509-10514.

Lee, C.Y., Tsai, J.L., Kuo, W.J., Yeh, T.C., Wu, Y.T., Ho, L.T., Hung, D.L., Tzeng, O.J. & Hsieh, J.C. 2004. Neuronal correlates of consistency and frequency effects on Chinese character naming: an event-related fMRI study. *Neuroimage*, 23, 4, 1235-1245.

Leroy, F., Glasel, H., Dubois, J., Hertz-Pannier, L., Thirion, B., Mangin, J. & Dehaene-Lambertz, G. 2011. Early maturation of the linguistic dorsal pathway in human infants. *The Journal of Neuroscience*, 26, 31(4), 1500-1506.

Leyfer, O.T., Tager-Flusberg, H., Dowd, M., Tomblin, B. & Folstein, S.E. 2008. Overlap between autism and specific language impairment: comparison of autism diagnostic interview and autism diagnostic observation schedule scores. *Autism Research*, 1, 284-296.

Makuuchi, M., Bahlmann, J., Anwander, A. & Friederici, A.D. 2009. Segregating the core computational faculty of human language from working memory. *Proceedings of the National Academy of Science*, 106, 20, 8362-8367

McCandliss, B.D. 2010. Educational neuroscience: The early years. *Proceedings of the National Academy of Science*, 107, 18, 8049-8050.

McClelland, J.L. & Rumelhart, D.E. 1981. An interactive activation model of context effects in letter perception: An account of basic findings. *Psychological Review*, 88, 375-407.

McCrory, E.J., Mechelli, A., Frith, U. & Price, C.J. 2005. More than words: A common neural basis for reading and naming deficits in developmental dyslexia? *Brain*, 128, 2, 261-267.

Meng, H., Smith, S.D., Hager, K., Held, M., Liu, J., Olson, R.K., Pennington, B.F., De-Fries, J.C., Gelernter, J., O'Reilly-Pol, T., Somlo, S., et al. 2005. DCD2 is associated with reading disability and modulates neuronal development in the brain. *Proceedings of the National Academy of Sciences*, 102, 47, 17053-17058.

Milne, D. & Santos, A. 2006. Understanding Subtypes of Dyslexia. *Journal of the Irish Learning Support Association*, 28: 43 – 61.

Milne, D. 2003. Sounding out blends & rimes. *Montessori International*, 69: 34 – 35.

Milne, D. 2005 Teaching the Brain to Read. SK Publishing, Berks, England.

Milne, D. 2013. How My Brain Learns to Read. Junior Learning, Auckland, New Zealand.

Milne, D., Hamm, J.P., Kirk, I.P., and Corballis, M.C. 2003. Anterior-posterior beta asymmetries in dyslexia during lexical decisions. *Brain and Language*, 84 (3), 309-317.

Milne, D., Nicholson, T. and Corballis, M.C. 2003. Lexical access and phonological decoding in adult dyslexic subtypes. *Neuropsychology*, 17 (3), 392-368.

Milne, D., Syngeniotis, A., Jackson, G. and Corballis, M.C. 2002. Mixed lateralization of phonological assembly in developmental dyslexia. *Neurocase*, 8, 205-209.

Montes, G. & Halterman, J.S. 2007. Psychological functioning and coping among mothers of children with autism: a population based study. *Pediatrics*, 119, 5, 1040–1046.

Morais, J., Bertelson, P., Cary, L. & Alegria, J. 1986. Literacy training and speech segmentation. *Cognition*, 24, 45-64.

Nicholson, T. 2000. Reading the writing on the wall. Debates, challenges and opportunities in the teaching of reading. Dunmore Press, Palmerston North, New Zealand.

Nicolson R.I., Fawcett A.J. 2011. Dyslexia, dysgraphia, procedural learning and the cerebellum. *Cortex*, 47, 1, 117-127.

Nicolson, R.I., Fawcett, A.J. & Dean, P. 2001. Developmental dyslexia: The cerebellar deficit hypothesis. *Trends in Neurosciences*, 24, 9, 508-511.

Parviainen, T., Helenius, P., Poskiparta, E., Niemi, P. & Salmelin, R. 2006. Cortical sequence of word perception in beginning readers. *Journal of Cognitive Neuroscience*, 26, 22, 6052-6061.

Paulesu, E., Demonet, J.F., Fazio, F., McCrory, E., Chanoine, V., Brunswick, N., Cappa, S. F., Cossu, G., Habib, M., Frith, C.D. & Frith, U. 2001. Dyslexia: Cultural diversity and biological unity. *Science*, 291, 5511, 2165-2167.

Pelli, D.G., Farell, B. & Moore, D.C. 2003. The remarkable inefficiency of word recognition. *Nature*, 423, 6941, 752-756.

Price, C.J., Wise, R.J.S., Warburton, E.A., Moore, C.J., Howard, D., Patterson, K., Frackowiak, R.S.J. & Friston, K.J. 1996. Hearing and saying. The functional neuro-anatomy of auditory word processing. *Brain*, 119, 919-931.

Racine, M.B., Majnemer, A., Shevell, M. & Snider, L. 2008. Handwriting performance in children with attention deficit hyperactivity disorder (ADHD). *Journal of Child Neurololology* 23, 4: 399-406.

Ramus, F. 2003. Developmental dyslexia: specific phonological deficit or general sensorimotor dysfunction? *Current Opinion in Neurobiology*, 13, 2, 212-218.

Ramus, F. 2004. Neurobiology of Dyslexia: A reinterpretation of the data. *Trends in Neurosciences*, 27, 12, 720-726.

Rapp, B. & Dufor, O. 2011. The neurotopography of written word production: an fMRI investigation of the distribution of sensitivity to length and frequency. *Journal of Cognitive Neuroscience*, 23, 12, 4067- 4081.

Ravizza, S., Anderson, J.R. & Carter, C.S. 2008. Errors of mathematical processing: The relationship of accuracy to neural regions associated with retrieval or representation of the problem state. *Brain Research*, 1238, 118-126.

Rayner, K., Foorman, B.R., Perfetti, C.A., Pesetsky, C.A., Pesetsky, D. & Seidenberg, M.S. 2001. How psychological science informs the teaching of reading. P*sychological Science in the Public Interest*, 2: 31-74.

Robinson, R. J. 1991. Causes and associations of severe and persistent specific speech and language disorders in children. *Developmental Medicine and Child Neurology*, 33, 943–962.

Rose, J. 2006. Independent review of the teaching of early reading. DfES, England.

Roux, F.E., Dufor, O, Guissani, C., Wamain, Y., Draper, L., Longcamp, M., et al. 2009. The graphemic/motor frontal area. Exner's area revised. *Annals of Neurology*, 66, 537-545.

Santos, A., Rondan, R., Milne, D., Démonet, J-F., & Deruelle, C. (2008). Social relevance boosts context processing in Williams syndrome. *Developmental Neuropsychology*, 33 (4), 1-12.

Santos, A., Milne, D., Rosset, D., & Deruelle, C. (2007). Challenging symmetry on mental retardation: Evidence from Williams syndrome. In E. B. Heinz (Ed.), *Mental Retardation Research Advances* (pp. 147-174). NY: Nova Science Publishers.

Saur, D., Kreher, B.W., Schnell, S., Kummerer, D., Kellmeyer, P., Vry, M.S., Umarova, R. et al. 2008. Ventral and dorsal pathways for language. *Proceedings of the National Academy of Science*, 105, 46, 18035-18040.

Schneider, H. & Eisenberg, D. 2006. Who receives a diagnosis of attention-deficit/ hyperactivity disorder in the United States elementary school population? *Pediatrics* 117, 4, 601-609.

Seymour, P.H., Aro, M. & Erskine, J.M. 2003. Foundation literacy acquisition in European orthographies. *British Journal of Psychology*, 94, 2, 143-174.

Share, D.L. 1995. Phonological recoding and self-teaching: sine qua non of reading acquisition. *Cognition*, 55, 151-218.

Shaywitz, B.A., Shaywitz, S.E., Pugh, K.R., Mencl, W.E., Fulbright, R.K., Skudlarski, P., Constable, R.T., Marchione, K.E., Fletcher, J.M., Lyon, G.R. & Gore, J.C. 2002. Disruption of posterior brain systems for reading in children with developmental dyslexia. *Biological Psychiatry*, 52, 2, 101-110.

Shaywitz, S. 2003. Overcoming Dyslexia. New York. Random House.

Shaywitz, S.E., Shaywitz, B.A., Pugh, K.R., Fulbright, R.K., Constable, R.T., Mencl, W.E., Shankweiler, D.P., Liberman, A.M. Skudlarski, P., Fletcher, J.M. et al. 1998. Functional disruption in the organization of the brain for reading in dyslexia. *Proceedings of the National Academy of Sciences*, 95, 5, 2636-2641.

Sherman, G.F, Galaburda, A.M. & Geschwind, N. 1985. Cortical anomalies in brain's of New Zealand mice: A neuropathologic model of dyslexia? *Proceedings of the National Academy of Sciences*, 82, 8072-8074.

Silani, G., Frith, U., Demonet, J.F., Fazio, F., Perani, D., Price, C., Frith, C.D. & Paulesu, E. 2005. Brain abnormalities underlying altered activation in dyslexia: A voxel based morphometry study. *Brain*, 128, 10, 2453-2461.

Simon, T.J. & Vaishnavi, S. 1996. Subitizing and counting depend on different attentional mechanisms: Evidence from visual enumeration in afterimages. *Perception & Psychophysics*, 58 (6), 915-926.

Simos, P.G., Fletcher, J.M., Bergman, E., Breier, J.I., Foorman, B.R., Castillo, E.M., Davis, R.N., Fitzgerald, M., & Papanicolaou, A.C. 2002. Dyslexia-specific brain activation profile becomes normal following successful remedial training. *Neurology*, 58, 8, 1203-1213.

Stein, J. 2001. The magnocellular theory of developmental dyslexia. *Dyslexia*, 7, 1, 12-36.

Swanson, J.M., Flodman P., Kennedy J., Spence, M.A., Moyzis, R., Schuck, S., Murias, M., Moriarity, J. et al. 2000. Dopamine Genes and ADHD. *Neuroscience and Biobehavioral Reviews*, 24, 1, 21-5.

Temple, E., Deutsch, G.K., Poldack, R.A., Millar, S.L., Tallal, P., Merzenich, M.M. & Galrieli, D.E. 2003. Neural deficits in children with dyslexia ameliorated by behavioral remediation: evidence from fMRI. *Proceedings of the National Academy of Science*, 100, 5, 2860-2865.

Torgerson, C.J., Brooks, G. & Hall, J.A. 2006. A systematic review on the use of phonics in the teaching of reading and spelling. Research Report RR711. DfES. England.

Ullman, M.T. & Pierpont, E.I. 2005. Specific language impairment is not specific to language: the procedural deficit hypothesis. *Cortex*, 41, 399-433.

Vinckenbosch, E. Robichon, F. & Eliez, S. 2005. Gray matter alteration in dyslexia: Converging evidence from volumetric and voxel-by-voxel MRI analyses. *Neuropsychologia*, 43, 3, 324-331.

Vinckier, F., Naccache, L. Papeix, C., Forget, J., Han-Barma, V., Dehaene, S. & Cohen, L. 2006. "What" and "where" in word reading: Ventral coding of written words revealed by parietal atrophy. *Journal of Cognitive Neuroscience*, 18, 12, 1998-2012.

Volkmar, F.R., State, M. & Klin, 2009. A. Autism and autism spectrum disorders: diagnostic issues for the coming decade. *Joural of Child Psychology and Psychiatry*. 50, 1, 108–15.

Ward, J., Sagiv, N. & Butterworth, B. 2009. The impact of visuo-spatial number forms on simple arithmetic. *Cortex*, 45, 1261-1265.

Warrington, E.K. & Shallice, T. 1980. Word-form dyslexia. *Brain*, 103, 99-112.

West, T.G. 1997. In the Mind's Eye: Visual thinkers, gifted people with dyslexia and other learning difficulties, computer images and the ironies of creativity. Amherst, New York: Prometheus Books.

Whalen, McCloskey, M., Lesser, R.P. & Gordon, B. 1997. Localizing arithmetic processing in the brain: Evidence from a transient deficit during cortical stimulation. *Journal of Cognitive Neuroscience*, 9, 3, 409-417.

Ziegler, J.C. & Goswami, U. 2005. Reading acquisition, developmental dyslexia, and skilled reading across languages: a psycholinguistic grain size theory. *Psychological Bulletin*, 131, 1, 3-29.

Junior Learning is committed to improving education for all learners by publishing books and other educational toys, games and technology applications.